Articles of Secession

How our systems would function (better) in an independent New Hampshire

Elliot "Alu" Axelman

Also by Alu Axelman

The Blueprint For Liberty
Presumed Guilty
The Plague That Must Not Be Questioned
The Progressive Solution
Taxation Is Theft
They Fear Unity
How Amazing Is The US Constitution?

Table of contents
Healthcare..5
National Defense..13
Law Enforcement..23
Interstate Travel..29
Currency...35
Taxes & Welfare...40
Energy..49
The Economy..55
Education..59
Federal Land...63
Public Support...68
Constitutionality..71

Introduction

This book will answer the most serious questions and concerns that pro-freedom individuals have when considering ideas regarding separating from the union and becoming a self-governing nation. We often hear people ask such questions as *"What would healthcare look like if we seceded?" "How might we survive without hospitals, insurance, or ambulances?" "What would law enforcement and national defense look like without governance?" "Which currency would we use?"* I hope that this pamphlet helps answer those questions.

If you have read 'The Blueprint For Liberty'[1], you surely understand that the union cannot remain intact. If you believe in freedom, you surely understand that the union should not remain intact, because the only remaining path to sustainable human freedom necessarily involves separation from DC and the union. That book focuses on the 'why'. This pamphlet will focus on the real, specific solutions regarding the 'how' of living in a thriving, prosperous Republic of New Hampshire after secession.

Healthcare

"What would healthcare look like in an independent New Hampshire once we leave the union?", a middle-aged woman asked from the crowd during the press conference for CACR32. I have been asked this question many times over the past few months, and it is a fair concern. Let's explore what healthcare in the Republic of New Hampshire may look like after the inevitable collapse of DC and the union.

Firstly, we must realize that once New Hampshire leaves the union, almost everything would remain the same as it is now. The sun would still rise in the east each morning. Paramedics and EMTs would staff ambulances, and patients would continue to see their doctors, as they always have. When children fall and sustain injuries, their parents will continue to bring them to urgent care centers or emergency rooms of hospitals, if the injury seems severe. Health insurance would still exist, just like it does today. There is no legitimate reason to believe that the sun would stop shining or that hospitals and ambulances would cease to exist if we cut ties with DC politicians. 99.99% of things would remain completely unchanged. There would be a few significant changes that would affect healthcare, however, and they would all be for the better.

1) Without DC politicians, regulators, and laws, individuals would be free from horrific laws such as the Obamacare law that literally punished[2] those who did not buy health insurance.

2) Without DC politicians, regulators, and laws, health insurance companies would be free to offer any plan they want, and individuals would be free to

purchase any plan they want. Some people may choose to buy lean health insurance plans that only cover catastrophes, while others may be willing to spend more for plans that give them more benefits. Currently, DC politicians and regulators use the threat of force to control exactly which types of plans health insurance companies in the united states are legally allowed to offer. There may be as many as millions of pages of federal laws[3] that dictate exactly which plans could legally be offered by "private" health insurance companies. Right now, it is federally illegal for health insurance companies to offer cheap plans to individuals. Secession would give Granite Staters much more freedom of choice.

3) Without DC politicians, regulators, and laws, it would become much easier for new medical facilities to open in New Hampshire. Currently, individuals who wish to open hospitals, clinics, surgical centers, labs, radiology centers, or other medical businesses may have to comply with millions of federal laws, codes and rules. In order to even ensure that they are in compliance, hospital boards are forced to hire many lawyers and other experts to comb through the infinite pages of federal laws to make sure that they are applying for all of the proper permits and to ensure that they are not violating any of the literally immeasurable[4] number of federal laws. As you might imagine, hiring lawyers and other compliance experts costs a lot of money. This federally imposed barrier makes it impossible for most people to open new facilities. Those who do successfully open a facility must spend massive sums of money on those experts, and they then pass on that cost to the customer (or the patient, in this case). Leaving the control of DC politicians could thus make healthcare

far less costly. With the majority of the barriers to opening new facilities now gone, we would see an explosion of new hospitals and clinics of all types. This competition would most likely lower costs and improve quality for patients.

4) Without DC politicians, regulators, and laws, bringing new drugs to market might be billions of dollars cheaper and decades quicker. On average, it takes 12-15 years and $2.6 billion[5] to have a new medication approved by the FDA. This harms and kills many patients. It also makes pharmaceutical companies spend massive amounts of money and time bringing drugs to market. They then have to pass this cost onto the customer, because if they can't make a profit, there would be no incentive for creating the medication in the first place. Without the FDA, medications in New Hampshire would likely be far less costly and move from conception to market far more expeditiously. Additionally, bringing new medications from conception to market might be upwards of 90% quicker, saving even more lives. Currently, the FDA[6] hurts many Granite Staters, yet we are forced by men with guns to pay $4 billion dollars annually to fund the FDA. Let's not even mention the incredible corruption[7] within the FDA and DC in general.

5) The federal government controls the reimbursement rates for Medicaid (taxpayer-funded insurance for the poor) and Medicare (taxpayer-funded insurance for the elderly). The Centers for Medicare & Medicaid Services (CMS) is perhaps the greatest reason for the harm to healthcare in the united states. Due to the federal government being 29 trillion in debt and having no money, they set the reimbursement rates for

Medicaid and Medicare extremely low. The rates likely depend on many factors but they seem to pay providers around 21-24% of the bill. So, when a person goes to the hospital for emergency surgery and receives a bill for $10,000, Medicaid may only pay around $2,100 to the hospital. The surgeons, anesthesiologists, nurses, techs, and everyone else in the hospital must be paid for their work, not to mention the equipment (ventilators, medications, etc.) used on the patient's procedures. $2,100 cannot even cover the costs that the hospitals spent on the patient, never mind making a profit. This happened on massive levels all over the united states for decades. Over the years, hospitals realized that they had to increase the prices of their medical bills because of the law reimbursement rates paid by CMS (which covers the majority of patients in the united states now, thanks to the federal government taking over the insurance market). Now, that same bill might be $50,000 despite only costing the hospital $10,000. And then CMS reimburses a fifth of $50,000, which is $10,000. Everyone is satisfied. Except for those with private health insurance. And especially those who choose not to have insurance. They have to pay $50,000 for a $10,000 procedure because the federal government distorted the market. This topic is extremely complicated and involves more federal government manipulation in the health insurance market than one could imagine. Needless to say, without the DC politicians meddling in the industry, healthcare and health insurance would be much less costly.

6) The tyrants in DC use CMS as a powerful tool to manipulate our behavior and coerce healthcare providers and hospitals into doing their bidding. Over the past few decades, they have convinced

nearly every provider in the union to accept Medicaid and Medicare. Now, the federal government has ruled that it has the power to force any provider who accepts CMS patients (takes any money from Medicaid or Medicare) into obeying even stricter laws. For instance, the federal government's highest court[8] recently ruled that the federal government does not have the power to force every business to force their employees to get the COVID vaccines *unless* the business accepts any CMS money. By accepting their money, you agree to follow pretty much any rules that DC tyrants create, even if Congress didn't pass a law to that effect.

7) Healthcare facilities generally do have to pay taxes, just like any other business. Some hospitals are exempt from some federal taxes if they meet certain criteria:

*"a tax-exempt hospital did not have to provide any free care to the poor so long as it maintained an emergency room open to all regardless of ability to pay, accepted **Medicare and Medicaid** patients, and had an independent governing body comprised of community leaders"*, as explained by TaxProf[9]. Thus, the federal government incentivizes hospitals to accept Medicare and Medicaid by lowering their taxes. Once the hospitals are hooked on CMS money, they have an extremely powerful tool to control them forever. The federal tax rate for businesses in the united states is 21% of net earnings. If a hospital in the united states earns a net of $1 million in a year, they must send $210,000 to the tyrants in DC right off the bat, under threat of force being used against them. Once we leave the union, this money would remain in the hospital. They could choose to lower costs for patients, give their staff raises, buy new equipment,

expand their facilities, or give charity to the community using that extra 21%. (Without federal payroll[10] taxes, healthcare businesses would save even more money, which would stay in New Hampshire and improve our communities)

8) Without the federal income tax, each individual provider (nurses, paramedics, doctors) may also save around 15-35% of their money each year. With every single provider in healthcare - and every other worker - in New Hampshire saving thousands of dollars per year, we would instantly become much more wealthy.

9) What about people who are currently on welfare because they are in poverty or disabled? In the free Republic of New Hampshire, people would work for a living. Any person with reasonable intelligence and physical health can easily find work and make a living by producing real value of some kind. In my experience, very few people receiving welfare are truly so severely disabled that they physically cannot earn a living. I would consider people to be completely disabled only if they have severe cerebral palsy or an equivalent disorder (bed-bound and on a ventilator) or if they are quadruple amputees who also cannot speak, for some reason. The fact is that anyone with one working limb or a functional larynx can earn a living. At the high end, we could imagine that there are around 500 people in New Hampshire who are completely disabled and physically cannot work for a living. Those few people (1 in every 2,700 people) would naturally be cared for by their family, friends, neighbors, or local churches or charity associations. This was the case before the government took on the role of charity collector and dispenser. Because in the eyes of those opposing

national divorce the united states would be as charitable and generous as New Hampshire is ruthless, the disabled people would only need to leave the state and enter Massachusetts and their every need would be cared for by the union.

As a worst case scenario, the people of New Hampshire would likely crowdsource a few dollars from their newfound savings of around 20-50k per year per worker in order to fund a facility for the truly disabled Granite Staters. I pledge to be the first one to donate if it comes down to it. In fact, I could probably fund the entire multi-million dollar facility without a nickel from taxes.

10) In 2021, federal regulations were changed regarding organ donation. DC politicians now require the organs from deceased people who are donors be allocated to the next person on the transplant list within a 250 nautical mile radius. This was a massive change from their prior policy, which called for the organ to go to the nearest person who needed it and then work in concentric outward circles. This allowed organ donors in New Hampshire to posthumously gift their organs to fellow Granite Staters if they pass away while a neighbor happens to need the organ in order to live. Now, nearly every organ from deceased Granite Staters will be sent to the highly populated areas like NYC, New Jersey, and even Philadelphia. If you or someone you love in New Hampshire is waiting for an organ, good luck waiting behind the 14 million people in the NYC metro area. Rep. Cambrils proposed a bill[11] to allow New Hampshire donors the option to prioritize their neighbors in New Hampshire if they pass away, which would save lives locally instead of sending an organ on a five hour

drive (which also decreases the chance of successful transplantation). Anti-freedom forces in DC are already fighting the bill and are hellbent on killing it. This is just one specific example of a niche healthcare area that would be much improved (totally solved) by secession from DC tyrants, who are literally dead set on stealing our organs.

11) What would the healthcare industry in New Hampshire look like five years after becoming independent?

Nobody could predict the future, but I have a few ideas: Without federal taxes and regulations, thousands of physicians, surgeons, nurses, PAs, midwives, and EMTs would pour into the state. Why not move to the most prosperous state AND enjoy the absence of ANY income tax? With the abolition of nearly every regulation on medical devices, many med-tech companies would likely relocate to New Hampshire from Silicon Valley, Israel, and Japan. Free-market surgical centers like the SCO[12] would likely become prevalent throughout the state within a few years. Without federal barriers, we might see a tripling in the number of hospitals, leading to lower costs and better care. Without the FDA and CDC indoctrinating our youth and adults into living on corn-syrup and Fauci-TV all day, they might exercise outside in the sunlight for a change, which could improve their health for a multitude of reasons. The list goes on....

I don't want to claim that it would be paradise, but living under the boot of DC tyrants sure seems pretty close to hell. We know we'd be MUCH better off without those sociopaths. Just how good will it be? Let's find out!

National Defense

Without the federal government, how would the tiny Republic of New Hampshire remain safe from foreign threats and hostile world powers? We would be living in the smallest country in the world, and we would not be able to afford any serious military, right?

While this is a valid question, the solution is relatively simple. I split it into two parts:

First, I remind skeptics that if we are to discuss threats to our survival, the government is by far the most dangerous one. Governments are responsible for nearly 100% of the murder committed in human history. Chinese dictators like Mao Zedong, Russian dictators like Stalin, the Kim family in North Korea, Castro in Cuba, Hitler in Germany, the list goes on. Even in the union, local governments kill thousands of people each year in 'police shootings' and the federal government massacred loads of innocent adults and children in the Waco, TX incident, interned Japanese Americans, and committed many more atrocities against humanity.

Additionally, the federal government makes its citizens less safe instead of making them safer, according to many experts[13]. The DC politicians regularly destabilize entire regions, infuriate entire populations (often by killing innocent children or placing embargos on innocent foreigners), and they often give billions of dollars worth of military training, weapons, and other equipment to the very worst terrorists and hostile regimes[14] in the world. The latest such example was the parting gift of 600,000 M16s, 2,000 armored vehicles, 40 aircraft,

4,702 Humvees, 162,000 pieces of communication equipment, and 16,000 night-vision goggles that the brilliant politicians from DC gave to the Taliban, one of the most vicious terrorist groups in the world. The gift was estimated at a value of over $20 billion[15] - which you were forced to pay for via federal taxes. Yes, your hard-earned money was used by DC politicians to buy M16 guns (which you are not allowed to own according to federal law) for the Taliban fighters. We must not forget that the most infamous terror group of the past decade - ISIS - was totally created[16] by the federal government when they trained rebels to overthrow a government only to find that those rebels were far from saints themselves, and would soon become ISIS.

It is hard to say for sure, but many believe that the federal government is a net detriment to our safety. The US military certainly could defend us from many hostile attacks and likely does act as a major deterrent to enemies, but they often arm the worst terrorists and oligarchs (including Putin and the CCP), destabilize regions, hurt innocent children, and royally mess up[17] defensive operations[18] in the homeland.

While foreign governments could theoretically dispatch their militaries to attack us, our own government already demonstrated that it can and will. In fact, nearly every opponent of allowing New Hampshire citizens to vote on independence cites the fact that the US military could and should roll in tanks[19] and kill us all as one of the primary reasons we should not peacefully separate from DC.

Make no mistake; hostile authoritarian governments such as China, Russia, Iran, and others surely would love to kill any vulnerable American. Their goal is to weaken the western culture of (diminishing, yet still somewhat existent) personal and economic freedom. So, how would an independent Republic of New Hampshire defend itself from the Chinese military?

As we mentioned previously, physical wars do not generally occur in the modern era. This is because:

1) the world's citizens have largely grown to support a civil and peaceful planet where humans can coexist without killing each other and

2) the weapons that the large nations possess are so devastating that the collateral damage would render nearly any attack counterproductive. Any nuclear bomb would kill or severely injure the entire population of North America and could cause injuries to nearly every human on Earth. If China were to attack a state, they would want to take it over and use its resources, right? If you blow up the whole state, it would be relatively useless to the attacker, and you will have just killed your would-be workers (or slaves).

The more effective attack would be one that captures the state's resources and/or people. The Chinese would love to take over our businesses and properties and enslave the people who live here. In order to do this, their military would have to physically invade the land. Even if they were well equipped and trained, they would face tremendous resistance, as mentioned previously. New Hampshire's citizens would enjoy homefield advantage and total decentralization, allowing for absolute guerilla warfare. No two units would have the same tactics or equipment. There would be no 'central command' to take over. Nearly every citizen would have an AR-15 or a long-range rifle, and there would be tanks and other powerful military equipment on the defending side, as well. Remember, New Hampshire already does have a military. It is called the 'National Guard', and it is the state's military. Tyrants from DC (especially Teddy Roosevelt) have thoroughly destroyed the link between National Guards and their states. By WW2, the National Guard was essentially part of the US military, and was deployed overseas, leading to the death of 175,000 State Militia soldiers. Today, there is practically no difference between National Guardsmen and US soldiers. Again, this is all the more reason we must take back our sovereignty from DC before it's too late.

The Guardsmen have been so intertwined with the US military that they have undergone the same training, much of which is focused on 'just following orders' without asking questions of superiors - there is no time to question orders in the middle of a battle! If New Hampshire did decide to peacefully withdraw from the union and govern itself, either the National Guard would remain loyal to its state and protect its citizens, or it would fight on behalf of the DC politicians, proving the most pessimistic secessionists right in the debate about state sovereignty.

Ideally, the Guardsmen would remain loyal to their neighbors. If not, we would naturally raise our own organized and semi-organized militias.

The Chinese soldiers would essentially have to go door to door killing each and every one of New

Hampshire's 1.4 million citizens, many of which look like this:

Would a foreign government really want to attack millions of these people on their own territory? What is to be gained by doing that?

Additionally, the state may already have a military alliance with Vermont, Maine, Massachusetts, and possibly the US military (if their divorce ended amicably). Of course, the more allies the sovereign state would have, the stronger their defensive capabilities would be - and the less likely any foreign military would be to risk invading in the first place.

"What about cyberattacks? China is already engaged in such warfare, are they not?"

Yes. China and other foreign governments likely are currently fighting us in the cyber-security realm. They surely spy on every state government on the planet (as does the federal government), and I do not trust them or any other government. This issue currently exists, though. It's not an issue that secession would create. Would a sovereign republic be in a better or worse position to handle cyber-attacks by foreign governments?

Again, decentralization answers this question for us. As Jacob taught us, *"don't put all your eggs in one basket"*. Currently, the DC politicians are doing us all a disservice. Our brilliant rulers leave all Americans very vulnerable to cyber attacks. How? If China wants to take over control of the united states - and thereby, to all of its people - all they need to do is hack one computer network located in Washington DC. Because the DC government has tremendous amounts of data (social security, birth certificate, wages, taxes, address, height, weight, race, relationships, etc.) on each and every person in the union, we are all extremely vulnerable to the ultimate cyber attack by a hostile government or terrorist group. If each of the 50 states were sovereign, like the founders intended them to be, China would have to hack 50 central computers in order to gain access to the same data (or to inject malware) on all Americans. If we decentralized even further - down to counties, cities, and eventually, to individuals - China would have to launch 330,000,000 individual successful cyber-attacks in order to overpower us technologically! THAT is the power of decentralization!

A sovereign New Hampshire would be in an even better position than most states, though. An incredible amount of our residents currently work in programming and/or cyber security. We also have one of the highest usage rates of cryptocurrencies per capita anywhere in the world. Once all federal regulations were lifted, New Hampshire would become even more prosperous, cyber-resilient, independent, untraceable, and uncontrollable.

Our foreign policy would likely be similar to Switzerland's. We would be neutral and mind our own business. We certainly would not inject ourselves into battles in Syria and Ukraine and Cuba. This would be a welcome change for our citizens after decades of suffering under a government that forced them to fund wars or military battles or operations in 196 countries around the world.

On the issue of finances, we have more good news. New Hampshire sends $15.3 billion dollars[20] to DC each year. The DC politicians send $3 billion to the state for its budget, plus some amount of money to individuals for welfare, plus some grants to local governments (like the funds for police to operate sobriety checkpoints, drones, and BEARcats). The highest estimate of the amount of money that DC sends to NH in total is $14.9 billion, which is $314 million less than we send them. Much of that money is Medicare, Medicaid, social security, TANF, SNAP, HUD, WIC, and other welfare programs. Individually, we would each save around 20-30% of our income once we no longer have to pay federal income taxes. All business owners would also enjoy keeping 21% more of their income. All other federal taxes would also not exist in New Hampshire anymore. But the tax savings would pale in comparison to the savings from deregulation. Currently, the immeasurable[21] number of federal regulations costs the union's economy far over $2 trillion[22] annually. Without burdensome regulations, the Republic of New Hampshire would likely become the most prosperous nation on the face of the Earth - by a long shot. Keep in mind that we already have the highest median household income in the union. Yes, we would easily be able to afford a sufficient military. We would not be the weakest country in the world. Not even close.

Would we be the smallest country in the world?

New Hampshire has 1.4 million residents. Monaco and Liechtenstein, two totally legitimate countries, both have under 40,000 residents. Gibraltar[23] has under 34,000 residents. Greenland has 56,000 residents. Grenada has 112,000. Belize has 400,000. Iceland has 341,000. New Hampshire would likely be tied with Estonia as the 80th smallest country in the world. We would likely be tied with Qatar for 7th place in GDP per capita. The united states would be in 9th place in the world with its $59,000 per capita GDP. It is hard to predict our total GDP once independent, but it might be somewhere in the middle of the pack due to our small size but incredible education, free market, and worth ethic.

To those who believe that our economy would suffer because the federal government would place a full embargo on all trading into or out of New Hampshire, keep in mind that an embargo is internationally considered an act of war. So, would the federal government declare war against Granite Staters for exercising their natural human right to a peaceful separation from an abuser? If they would be that cruel, they would only prove our point – they are evil and abusive.

Additionally, an embargo on New Hampshire would seek to starve not only everyone in New Hampshire, but it would also completely cut off Maine from the rest of the union. While it is possible, an embargo is very unlikely. But if we had to live on our own resources for some time, we could certainly do so.

I address the potential outcomes of a military attack on peaceful New Hampshire citizens by the federal government in a little more detail in 'The Blueprint For Liberty'[24].

Another issue that seems difficult to reconcile is the current nuclear arsenal owned by the US military. Again, it may not be much of an issue after all. The two options are: The US military keeps all nuclear arms, or they give the New Hampshire military roughly one fiftieth of the nuclear arms. In the worst case scenario, the federal government would retain all of its nuclear weapons. The citizens of New Hampshire are extremely peaceful and are not very paranoid. We understand that there is a nearly zero percent chance that the federal government would use nuclear weapons in New Hampshire or anywhere else within a thousand miles of the continent, because such an action would kill or severely injure hundreds of millions of people, including DC politicians.

If we are going to compare the potential harm of foreign and domestic threats in regards to independence, we must address another very important fact: Currently, the single biggest threat to regular citizens is the federal government! They are the ones who violate us. They regularly steal our money, spy on us, abuse us, control us, and threaten us. If we are going to do a cost/benefit analysis of separation, we must also consider that the single biggest threat to our safety, liberty, and property would be eliminated if we were to separate from DC politicians permanently.

On a somewhat related note, I would like to address one of the most common objections to peaceful separation from DC. *"Soldiers fought and died to preserve the union! Splitting up the union would disgrace their memories and make their sacrifices be in vain!"* If soldiers died for any noble principle, it surely was human liberty, not the perpetual continuation of a monstrous centrally-controlled union of semi-states regardless of the tyranny and discontent. The soldiers sacrificed their lives so that we could be free to live as we please, with free speech and arms and property rights and due process and all other types of freedom. However, the DC politicians are increasingly destroying those freedoms and violating our natural rights. Any soldier who supports freedom must surely support separating from the most dangerous tyrants to you and me. In fact, the NH Independence PAC[25] was spontaneously formed in the summer of 2022 by two pro-secession residents who both happen to be veterans!

Law enforcement

What would law enforcement look like in the Republic of New Hampshire?

A friend of mine asked me that question on the day of the historic hearing on CACR32, the legislation that would place the question of independence on the ballot if passed by the legislature. She supports liberty and state independence, but she was seriously concerned that we may not have any police if we cut ties with DC.

The answer to the question is quite simple: When New Hampshire secedes, law enforcement will operate exactly as it does now. Actually, it will have a few minor changes. And all of them would make policing in New Hampshire much more pleasant for the officers and the citizens.

For those who are not yet aware, the New Hampshire state police are funded by state taxes, and local police are primarily funded by local (town and city) taxes with some grants by the state government. Leaving the union would not affect this basic funding mechanism. A miniscule portion of the money used for police operations in New Hampshire does come from DC, though.

In 2017, the DOJ sent $500,000 in taxpayer money from DC to New Hampshire police departments, reportedly to help them hire more officers[26].

In 2019, the DHS sent $75,000 in taxpayer money from DC to the Portsmouth Police[27] Department so that they could buy surveillance drones[28]. *"Some of the drones will have a powerful 30X zoom camera,* which will allow a drone to surveil a place without the suspect knowing it's there, and a thermal imaging camera that will allow police to easily locate suspects in some cases.", as reported by Patch.com. The Portsmouth Police Department now has eight drones. Do you think that we could survive without being surveilled by government drones? I am sure that we would thrive without them.

In 2014, the DHS sent $258,000 in taxpayer money from DC to the Concord Police Department to buy a BEARcat[29], a military-style tank-vehicle hybrid. Do you think that we could survive without being terrorized by government military vehicles? I am sure that we would thrive without them.

All sobriety checkpoints[30] conducted by police in New Hampshire are funded by 'federal highway funds', according to the state government's website. Do you think that we could survive without being violated by illegal and due-process-violating sobriety checkpoints that will necessarily presume all drivers to be drunk until they prove that they are sober? I am sure that we would thrive without them.

Once New Hampshire severs ties with DC, it would be very unlikely for New Hampshire's cops to work in joint operations with federal agents, such as the CBP, ICE, FBI, ATF, and all other federal agencies. Over the past few years, local and state cops have worked on joint efforts with federal law enforcement to conduct:

1) Due-process-violating immigration checkpoints in middle of the state

2) Due-process-violating asset forfeiture[31] (stealing property from innocent Granite Staters without convicting them of any crime)

3) A massive raid on 'the crypto six', a group of Keene residents charged with various federal crimes related to using crypto-currency. The innocent individuals are currently being punished, despite not being convicted yet. They are facing decades in prison if convicted of all of the crimes they are being charged with. None of the charges involve any crimes in which there were any actual victims

Do you believe that we could survive without federal agents working with local and state cops to accomplish the above tasks? I am sure that we would thrive without them.

Another change would allow police officers to be held accountable for violating civil rights of citizens. Currently, a federal doctrine called 'qualified immunity' makes it impossible to sue police officers for violating your civil rights unless you can prove that they knew that they were violating a civil right that was previously established by a court case with the exact same set of circumstances as your case. The federal government created the doctrine of 'qualified immunity' and then extended the protection to state and local government officials. Once we leave the union, this doctrine will no longer protect police from being held accountable in court.

Once we leave the union, federal drug laws would not apply. The DEA would never again break into someone's home to search for drugs. The war on drugs would likely end immediately or gradually within a few years after secession.

In the broader sense, nearly every violation of due process has roots in DC. Much like asset forfeiture, eminent domain[32] (the government taking your property for 'public use') is a federal doctrine that DC politicians extended to state and municipal governments. Without ties to DC, both of those forms of legalized theft by police disappear.

Additionally, police officers in New Hampshire would become much happier, which benefits them, their families, and their communities. In addition to being relieved from no longer being required to participate in a tyrannical system, every cop would save around 25% of their income due to the abolition of the income tax. Considering that all other federal taxes (including the 21% tax on businesses) and regulations would no longer exist, every person in society would be much more prosperous.

In summary, nothing would change about our law enforcement operations in New Hampshire - except that it would become substantially better, less tyrannical, and more accountable. I could live with that.

Prisons
All jails and prisons within New Hampshire will continue to operate after secession exactly as they did when we were part of the union. There is a medium-security federal prison and a minimum-security federal prison camp in Berlin, New Hampshire. Only 587 total federal prisoners reside in them, according to PrisonerResource.com[33]. It is impossible to predict exactly what the state police and/or attorney general would negotiate with DC, but these prisoners would likely be transferred to other federal prisons or to other state prisons.

None of those scenarios would be terribly difficult or unusual. The only part of the transition that may not be extremely quick and easy might be the state of New Hampshire's government formally buying the federal prison property from the federal government. Assuming the property is owned by DC, this sale may cost New Hampshire some money. Exactly how negotiations would go or what they would entail is anybody's guess. The state and local penitentiaries would continue to operate as they did before the split.

Courts

Within New Hampshire, there are federal, state, and county courts. The state and county courts would continue to operate as they always have. The federal courts would no longer operate within the borders of New Hampshire. The state government would likely buy the federal court buildings from the federal government. The justice systems within New Hampshire would continue to prosecute crimes as before. The federal government, courts, and agents would no longer have any jurisdiction within New Hampshire. This would mean that federal crimes would no longer exist. Unless prohibited by state law, Granite Staters would be able to smoke cannabis while buying suppressors for their machine guns using their favorite cryptocurrency, if that's what they desired.

Fire, water, trash, and other utilities

A surprising number of people have expressed concerns about how fire departments and other municipal systems would function once New Hampshire leaves the union. This is such a simple answer that we cannot dedicate a whole chapter to answering it. Even more so than law enforcement, fire departments will remain almost completely unchanged. The only potential changes may involve fewer federal regulations, allowing firefighters more flexibility and freedom. However, most fire departments would likely continue to adhere to national and international firefighting standards, because they are regulated by non-governmental associations which credential fire departments, and because they keep the firefighters and their communities safe. There may be some small losses from occasional federal grants. The biggest change will likely be the elimination of the federal income tax, which would allow the average firefighter in New Hampshire to keep an extra 20-30 percent of their income. Municipal systems such as garbage collection, water & sewer maintenance, and many others would likely remain even more unchanged than fire departments.

Interstate Travel

"Once New Hampshire secedes, will we be able to travel to other states?"

This is certainly a legitimate question. Many people rightfully fear that once we cut ties to DC, they may not be able to travel to other states for work or pleasure. Of course, many New Hampshire citizens do work in Massachusetts, Maine, and Vermont. Many also travel to other states to see family or for vacations. If secession meant that citizens were trapped in New Hampshire forever or that it would be extremely difficult to travel to other states, it would certainly be a reason to support secession less or not at all.

While it is not possible to predict the future or guarantee any political outcome, we could be fairly certain of how interstate travel might play out once New Hampshire inevitably cuts ties with DC politicians. As with all interstate lines, both sides have the right to control the border. Let's address New Hampshire and the union:

New Hampshire
The state is increasingly run by libertarians, especially on issues involving borders. By the time secession occurs, the majority of the legislature and the electorate will likely be libertarian, at least on border issues. Over the past few decades, progressives have been growing bolder in their declarations that borders should not exist anywhere on Earth for any reason whatsoever. So, the progressives in the legislature would certainly endorse a totally open border policy with the union. If they believe that there should be no border

separating the United states from Mexico or Canada, they would surely not want any border separating Vermont, Maine, and Massachusetts from New Hampshire. The Republicans in the legislature are governing more like libertarians each year, and most of them seem to be fairly liberal on border issues. Considering their support for free trade and prosperity, we could safely assume that they would not build a wall or implement strong immigration controls on New Hampshire's borders. Once they mentioned that it would cost taxpayers money to do so, the ultra-frugal tax base would likely reject the proposal anyway. The moderates in the legislature also seem to be quite liberal on border policy. It seems unlikely that they would support strong immigration controls with union states either. In summary, there would be little to no appetite for blocking travel anywhere in the New Hampshire legislature.

The union
The united states and DC are increasingly controlled by progressives. And one of the hallmarks of progressive ideology is the belief that borders are nothing more than a modern construct related to authoritarianism and racism, and that they should not exist. Most states are run by progressives, especially on border policies. Moderate Republicans in DC also support open borders, and they generally do not oppose Democrat policies. Centrists in both parties support open borders. The few conservatives in Congress who support moderate to strong border controls are diminishing in numbers and strength. And those conservatives would be unlikely to support policies that choke out the libertarian-conservative state of New Hampshire. Blocking travel from New Hampshire would also

mean blocking or severely restricting travel from the entire state of Maine, as well. It would be very difficult to imagine Congress blocking travel to and from Maine and New Hampshire. Considering that the federal government and nearly every state in the union has been increasingly supporting freedom of movement all over the world, blocking travel from New Hampshire would be hypocrisy so profound that even politicians would not likely endorse it.

What would daily life look like for residents of Manchester who commute to Boston every day for work?

There would likely be no restrictions from New Hampshire's side of the border. And the progressives who run Massachusetts and Boston have made it clear that they do not believe in borders, so they could not possibly restrict the worker's commute to and from work. It would be hard to imagine any restrictions for the Granite Stater. Traveling to Vermont or Maine would also likely be unrestricted. And traveling for pleasure would likely be as easy as traveling for work. While New Hampshire license plates would no longer be 'united states' plates, the most likely scenario would presume that the federal government and other states would respect the license of New Hampshire drivers, just like they do for drivers from Canada. Currently, drivers with licenses and plates from Ontario, Quebec, and all other Canadian provinces are able to drive around the united states without any issues[34], and vice versa.

Likewise, residents of the union states would be free to travel into New Hampshire as often as they desire. I could not imagine anyone stopping them. We are very welcoming, and we love when people visit our state, especially if they are spending money here.

"How would air travel be affected once New Hampshire is independent?"

Many Granite Staters rely on airline service to bring them to faraway destinations, whether for business or pleasure. Let's explore how air travel might be affected by New Hampshire's independence.

Firstly, it is important to understand that very little will be noticeably different when traveling on an airline from a traveler's perspective. If you have a favorite air carrier, such as Southwest or Delta, you will still be able to use your well-earned miles and travel on those airlines. In New Hampshire, we have two large airports that offer airline service, Manchester Regional, and Pease Air Force Base, both of which offer tickets from a selection of a dozen or so airlines. In this case, nothing would be different when you purchase your ticket, so long as these airlines still serve these airports. If you have ever flown internationally, you understand the process, and it is pretty simple.

History tells us that less regulation on airlines results in greater competition and a decrease in ticket prices. Before the Airline Deregulation Act of 1978, the Civil Aeronautics Board (CAB) controlled how the airlines operated. *"Under the Civil Aeronautics Board system, routes were supposed to be awarded among the existing carriers based on the perceived needs of the communities and cities requiring service ... This [control] produced a system that was not designed to be cost-efficient, but it was stable[35]."*

Since routes had to be approved by the Civil Aeronautics Board, very few, if any, were ever approved. The other issue was that the Civil Aeronautics Board set fares and rates too high for many average citizens to afford. The initial shake-up and talk of deregulation began in the early 1970s with economist Alfred Kahn. Kahn's background as an economist echoes his understanding that we should view the airlines in a business structure, rather than as a public utility to be centrally controlled by DC politicians. He figured that if we broke up the airline industry structure, new airlines would emerge, which would, in turn, lower the fares and increase competition[36]. Before the Act even passed, Kahn attacked regulation of the airlines in order to create something as close to total deregulation as the existing law would permit . . . *"we're going to get the airline eggs so scrambled that no one was ever going to be able to unscramble them."*[37]

Today, the united states offers the Open Skies Agreement for international airlines, which would take effect flying from the union to New Hampshire. According to the US Department of State[38], 'Open Skies' agreements are bilateral air service agreements the federal government negotiates with other countries to provide rights for airlines to offer international air services. They are pro-consumer, pro-competition, and pro-growth, and include reciprocal obligations to eliminate government interference in commercial airline decisions about routes, capacity, and pricing. This effect reduces overall consumer pricing while maintaining efficiency and facilitating economic growth. Negotiating between international routes becomes more straightforward with Open Skies agreements.

George W. Bush organized the Department of Homeland Security, which led to the creation of our beloved Transportation Security Administration (TSA). Anyone who has flown on a commercial airline knows the pains of the "new and improved" airport security and the long lines and bodily violations that go with it. Before September 11, 2001 and the creation of the TSA, security generally involved a metal detector, and your family and friends were allowed to enter the gate area to see you off. Gone are the days of saying goodbye without having your personal space violated by these agents and machines and your water bottle or nail clipper taken hostage. It is interesting to note that airports are not required to hire the national TSA. Our airports could employ their own security companies or system if they prefer. However, the government taxes us for the TSA anyway, so utilizing their security service is the financially wise decision.

When Joe Biden took office in 2020, he made it mandatory that anyone on federal property wears a mask due to the ongoing COVID-19 pandemic. This mandate is still in effect two years later, which means anyone at an airport within the union must adhere to this rule. Unfortunately, it is primarily the airlines that enforce the mask rules, so it is unlikely that the independence of New Hampshire would have much effect on this ruling. On the other hand, if there were domestic travel within the Republic of New Hampshire, the mask mandate would no longer apply. We can assume the same would be true if vaccination were a prerequisite to travel by air in the united states.

***The above article was co-authored by Katie Guello

Currency

If New Hampshire cut ties to DC and no longer participated in the union, what would we use for currency?

Many people have asked this question, and some have openly admitted to being afraid of how we would function as a society without using 'the mighty dollar'.

What exactly is currency?

Many people live their entire lives without giving much thought to the definition or history of currency. Simply explained, currency developed naturally as a medium of exchange in order to facilitate trade among people[39] for products and services. Currency could be thought of as a receipt, which denotes services rendered or stored value that could be exchanged for a predetermined amount of product or service. Without these receipts, employers would have to pay their employees with their product, which could make it difficult for the employee to trade in the marketplace. Money simplifies and facilitates trade within a society. A video[40] explains this concept quite well. Indeed, the last 15 seconds of the video is crucial to understanding the currency that was created by a group of truly sinister politicians and bankers in 1910 and solidified by FDR in 1933 and Nixon in 1971[41].

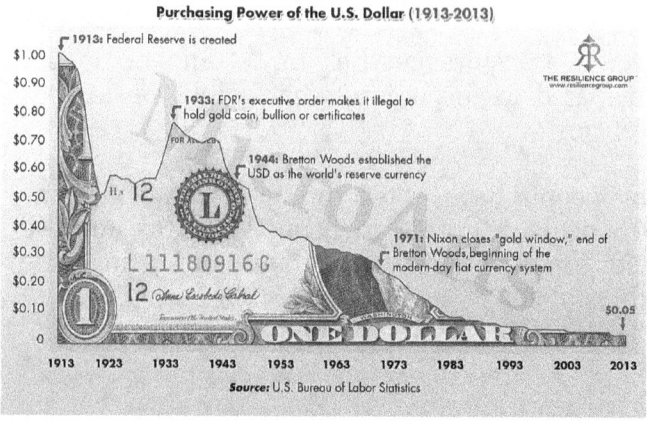

Before corrupt politicians and bankers created their joint venture in the 20th century, dollars in the united states represented real gold, which the federal government was obligated to grant the 'bearer of the bill upon demand'. In 1910, however, a then-secret meeting between bankers and politicians who were involved in 'banking regulation' met and created a banking cartel, which would be partnered with and supported by the federal government. Three years after drawing up their plan, these authoritarians passed the Federal Reserve Act. The federal reserve was a bank that could loan non-existent money to the federal government, which the federal government could then spend. Naturally, this caused massive inflation. The author of the book 'the creature from Jekyll Island' explains how inflation benefits the government and big banks[42] while harming regular citizens.

In 1933, President Franklin D. Roosevelt criminalized the ownership of gold and demanded that all

Americans hand over their gold to the federal reserve (whose board is selected by the president of the united states). This began the authoritarian, corrupt transition away from the gold standard that had backed the dollar. Now that the federal reserve - the joint venture between the united states government and the most powerful bankers of the era - owned nearly all of the gold in the union, FDR could really put a dagger in the heart of American currency. In 1934, King Roosevelt declared that gold shall cost $35 per ounce[43]. For the first time, the government had fixed the price of gold to the dollar, preventing the free market from discovering and setting the exchange rate. Since then, we have not had anything resembling a free market in the united states. This socialist/fascist president showed the American people the simplest example of authoritarian government control of the currency. And his sycophants continued to reelect him again and again. The federal government continued to empower the Federal Reserve and continued to solidify their partnership with the banking cartel. In 1971, Republican president (and infamous crook) Richard Nixon officially moved the dollar off of the gold standard, putting the final nails in the coffin of America's national currency.

Even the united states government[44] readily admits that you would have to spend over $2,580 today to buy the same things that just $100 would buy in 1913. This translates to an inflation rate of over 2500% since the establishment of the federal reserve in 1913. If you open your wallet and look at those paper bills, you'll notice that they say 'federal reserve note'. If you look at bills from before the creation of the federal reserve, that phrase does not exist. Instead, you might find phrases like 'silver certificate', 'united states note', 'dollars' and 'gold coin' and 'treasury note', depending on the era.

An increasing number of Americans are realizing that federal reserve notes have decreasing value with each passing day. Current inflation is between seven[45] and 20 percent[46] per year and will likely continue to accelerate in the coming years.

So, the DC politicians' currency is anything but 'mighty'.

That said, once we leave the union, Granite Staters would likely find that the choice of currency would not be an issue. We would have plenty of options. We could continue using dollars, because nothing would stop us from continuing to do what we've been doing for our entire lives. There is no reason to believe that our legislature would suddenly pass a law prohibiting the use of dollars. People in countries around the world use the dollar, and there is no reason why we could not do so regardless of whether we remain in the union.

For those who prefer to use money that doesn't constantly decrease in value, gold[47] and silver are great and are already used quite frequently in New

Hampshire. Many businesses and individuals regularly trade 'goldbacks', bill-like gold notes with exact amounts of gold content contained inside of them. Additionally, crypto-currencies are used more widely in New Hampshire than any other state in the union, it seems. Even if we had to transition away from the dollar, it would not be as painful or radical as people might imagine. We already have an excellent infrastructure of alternative currencies in place. It simply would not be an issue.

Taxes & Welfare

"Will we throw grandma out of the nursing home?"

That exact question was asked by a state legislator during the historic first public hearing in a legislative body on the question of independence in at least 160 years. While it may sound extreme, it is a reasonable question.

Many New Hampshire citizens are concerned about what will happen to retired and incapacitated individuals in New Hampshire once we separate from the union. Some people erroneously believe that all welfare comes from DC. It is important to keep in mind that while some welfare does come from DC, all of the money they sent to the state governments and to individuals was first taken by force from Americans via federal taxes. So, at best, the DC politicians are stealing our money and then giving it back to us (minus costs of administration and other expenditures). Let's address the largest welfare programs:

Social Security is a federal program that is funded by a 6.2% tax on income and another 6.2% tax on payroll (the employer must pay this to DC whenever they pay their employees). Social security alone causes the DC politicians to receive $12.40 for each $100 paid to employees anywhere in the united states. The employee and employer must each also pay 1.45% for the federal Medicare tax, bringing the total taxation to 15.3% for Social Security and Medicare[48]. This is totally separate from the income tax, which has tiered rates that range from 10% to 37%. If the average employee has an effective federal income tax rate of 20%, this means that DC politicians take 35.3% of every dollar paid to employees in the union via income/FICA taxes alone. Keep in mind that all of this ceases to exist once New Hampshire secedes. Considering that all other federal taxes and regulations would disappear, workers would be considerably wealthier after the separation from DC.

Contrary to what some fear-mongers have claimed during the debate on whether to place the question of independence on the ballot, individuals who pay into Social Security are entitled to receive their money back even if they move out of the union. According to SSA.gov[49], DC cannot send Social Security checks to North Korea or Cuba, for obvious reasons. Those who reside in one of those countries are eligible to receive their checks once they move to another country.

Medicaid is a state program that is heavily funded by DC via federal tax dollars. New Hampshire may choose to abolish the program after secession, but that would be a separate issue entirely. Secession would not cause Medicaid or any other state program to disappear.

Federal programs such as SNAP, HUD, WIC, and TANF would likely not give welfare to citizens of the Republic of New Hampshire. As we discuss in the article on healthcare, few (if any) working-age humans truly need welfare due to the physical inability to work (quadruple amputee). Additionally, any person who did feel strongly about their desire to continue living in a state with robust welfare programs would be free to move to any other state in the union in order to continue living their lives as they always have.

Let's get back to the case of 'grandma in a nursing home'.

Ideally, the secession negotiations would include a provision that stipulates that all persons who paid into Medicare for more than two decades and who are now relegated to live in a nursing home shall continue to receive the same Medicare coverage that they received before secession for the remainder of their lives. Realistically, these people did pay into the system with the expectation that they would receive Medicare, and they can no longer work.

It is possible that the DC politicians would admit that they do not care about letting the elderly die and that they do not care that they agreed to cover them with Medicare that they paid into. If DC politicians cut off Medicare and other federal welfare programs from the old lady in the nursing home, the burden would fall onto the residents of New Hampshire. Currently, we are already an extremely generous people. We give large amounts of charity and we spend a lot of time volunteering to help the needy. Once we become much more prosperous due to the elimination of all federal taxes and regulations, we would likely have an average of anywhere from $20,000 to $80,000 more in our pockets each year. Keep in mind that federal regulations cost the economy well over 2 trillion dollars each year. All of them would cease to exist in New Hampshire, unleashing economic freedom and prosperity at levels never seen before. These people would surely contribute enough money, volunteering, and other resources to help ensure that the old lady in the nursing home is well cared for.

It is likely that each person could save money for retirement, earn a pension from a private company, or have family who could ensure that they are properly cared for as they age. In worst-case scenarios in which a person has no money, retirement fund, pension, or family, the neighbors, churches, and other charity organizations would step in and help. While some Marxists claim that Americans are super greedy, the facts show that Americans donated over $410 billion[50] in 2018. It is not likely that grandma would be thrown out of the nursing home or that anyone would starve in New Hampshire.

Many people have expressed concerns about the state raising taxes to make up for the federal taxes and welfare going away once we separate from DC. One Representative said that secession is the quickest path to a state income tax and state sales tax (New Hampshire currently has neither). This is a reasonable concern.

What if New Hampshire's state and local governments could continue to provide all of the services they currently provide while drastically lowering – and possibly even eliminating – all taxation[51] in the state?

There are a few revenue-raising programs that the New Hampshire government already uses:

Lottery
Like every other state in the union, the NH government operates a lottery system. Many stores throughout the state sell the state government's lottery tickets. A quarter of the gross proceeds go to the state budget for education. This program has

contributed nearly $2 billion[52] to the state's education budget since its inception in 1964. Unlike taxation/extortion which is collected using the threat of violence or prison, people purchase lottery tickets of their own volition – whenever they feel like it!

If the government operates more lotteries, improves its efficiency, or spends less money each year, this revenue stream could fund a large portion of the state government's annual budget.

Fee for service
The New Hampshire government currently operates 82 liquor stores around the state. Since the prices and products are attractive & tax-free and since the selection is large, consumers voluntarily give their money to the government stores in exchange for liquor and wine products. The NH Liquor & Wine stores earned $160 million[53] in profits in 2016.

The NH state government and local governments operate many programs. These programs should fund themselves by simply charging a fee for their usage. This is the basic premise of tolls. If the government wants our money for a service or product, they should play fairly like the rest of society does. They should earn our money.

Bonds
The US government, state governments, and local governments ask for loans from citizens, much like citizens ask for loans from banks. Governments do this by selling 'bonds'. When a government needs money for a project, they borrow money from individuals for a set interest rate. They sell a 'bond' to anyone willing to buy it. The bond has a set

timeline and a set interest rate. The bond holder receives regular interest payments and gets his principal investment back when the bond matures. The government gets a loan (without coercion) and the citizen lender gets a predictable interest rate on their investment. Everyone wins and nobody is coerced. Why don't bonds totally fund all government budgets? If people believe in the government and/or want to help support it, they will support it financially. If nobody trusts or likes the government...maybe it should change its ways.

Advertising
In addition to all of the charity that is given by NH residents, at least three societal functions of New Hampshire are currently funded voluntarily.

In partnership with the NH Dept. of Transportation, the 'Adopt-A-Highway' program maintains highways using volunteers and funds generated via advertising. Simply put, businesses pay a few hundred dollars per month or supply volunteers for cleanup in exchange for their company name being shown on a sign along the highway. The business receives advertising, the highway remains clean, and nobody is robbed of their hard earned money.

Currently, Subway, McDonald's, Dunkin Donuts, IHOP, Denny's, Whole Foods, Weight Watchers, AAA, Hampton Inn, Waste Management, and many other companies voluntarily do business with Adopt-A-Highway in exchange for advertising. Evidently, these businesses see value in this exchange. If they did not want to spend money on the program, they wouldn't. When we voluntarily transfer our money to another party, we are inherently affirming that we see more value in the product or service we receive than in the money we pay for it. When you spend a dollar on a coffee, you are essentially telling the cashier that you want the coffee more than you want that dollar bill. When one party uses violence or threatens to use violence, this exchange becomes unbalanced and is no longer moral.

Cleverly utilizing buses[54], bus stops, and their websites[55] as space for advertising, the Nashua and Manchester transit authorities receive money from businesses that want to place their advertisement in front of hundreds of thousands of commuters. Manchester encourages businesses to 'Adopt A Site'[56] in the city, as well.

Companies spend nearly 200 billion[57] dollars per year on advertising in the united states. Why wouldn't governments want to receive their 'fair share' of that gold mine? If that isn't enough incentive, maybe abolishing mandatory, unethical, and inherently violent taxation could encourage the government to step into the future of revenue generation.

Governments could take the concept of advertising a step further, though. Utilizing the same revenue model as millions of YouTube creators, podcasters, and talk-show hosts, they could sell ads in various ways. If they allowed YouTube, for example, to host House and Senate sessions every day, the US government could probably earn billions of dollars[58] a year in ad revenue due to the millions of views such videos would receive. If a child reviewing toys on YouTube earns $22 million a year[59] from ad revenue, I'm sure the federal government - a collection of the 600 (more like four million) most brilliant people on

Earth could easily generate a few trillion dollars a year. Keep in mind that the annual budget for the entire federal government is only around $5 trillion a year. If our 'leaders' made a real attempt to – or if they were forced to – they could replace taxation with passive income from ads.

We could take the concept a step further, though! Although we might already fund the whole US government without any taxes, our elected officials could generate surplus money which could be given to the truly needy or to those who have been paying $20,000 to Uncle Sam every year for decades. As we've learned from billboards and some government ad sales, any space that is viewed a lot can be utilized (rented out) to advertisers for serious money. Why are the inner and outer walls of every capitol building plain white? Why aren't they generating passive revenue for the government to fund its services? Could you imagine how much Musk or Bezos would pay each year to advertise on such prime real estate?? The government could put every square inch of its property up for bid and raise trillions of dollars without taxation and without violating anyone's consent!

"That's great, Alu. But the state budget is like six billion dollars per year. The NH government could never raise that much money voluntarily!", argues the pessimist.

The budget could easily be trimmed by a few billion dollars if NH politicians would stop promising to redistribute our hard earned money to those who choose not to work. It could be trimmed by another $1.5 billion if the state government stopped funding government schools (don't worry, local governments in NH still spend $3 billion per year on government schools. Ending the forcible redistribution of wealth (welfare) would shave another $500 million per year from the state budget.

Thirdly, the NH government could reasonably raise $6 billion per year by utilizing and expanding upon the methods outlined above.

Fourthly, If the citizens felt that politicians were appropriately using the money they were entrusted with, surely they would donate to the government when they feel it is necessary. If these methods of revenue generation fall short of the proposed budget, there is nothing stopping New Hampshire residents (who happen to be the richest in the nation) from voluntarily writing a check to the state government to close the fiscal gap!

Energy Policy

What would energy production and consumption look like in an independent state of New Hampshire?

Currently, New Hampshire residents consume around 320 trillion BTU of energy per year. The Seabrook nuclear power plant provided 59% of New Hampshire's 2020 in-state electricity net generation, according to EIA.gov[60]. The rest of our energy is produced via coal, gas, oil, solar, wind, and hydroelectric, and possibly other forms methods. At 21 cents per kw/h[61], it is currently one of the most expensive states for energy. However, it is roughly average for New England. New Hampshire consumes more energy than it produces, making it a net importer of energy. Thus, some pessimists believe that independence is totally impossible for New Hampshire.

First, we must address the many reasons[62] a rapidly growing number of Granite Staters are supporting independence from the union. We understand that we are in a brutal, abusive relationship with DC politicians, and the abuse is increasing each day and showing no signs of stopping. We have tried every manner of recourse, including voting, lawsuits, petitions, and protests. Nothing has made DC politicians stop violating our natural rights, from property rights to the right to peace, and from privacy to the right to bodily autonomy and due process. When someone is in an abusive relationship, they do not need the perfect long-term plan in order to leave their abuser. When a woman is being beaten viciously by her husband, she runs away at the first opportunity she finds. She may end up sleeping on her friend's couch and eating junk for a week, but that is still better than being abused. When we discuss leaving the terrible relationship with DC politicians, we must not compare an independent New Hampshire to utopia. We must compare it to the status quo. And currently, we are miserable because we are forced to pay 4 trillion dollars per year in order to fund our own abuse.

Federal regulations
Once New Hampshire declares independence from DC politicians, its people would no longer have to concern themselves with federal laws, regulations, or taxes. First, this means that each worker in New Hampshire would save around 15-30% of their income each year. This would allow them to buy the same amount of energy even if it became substantially more expensive. But it wouldn't. It would likely become much more abundant and much cheaper. Currently, the largest hurdle to opening a new power plant is the federal regulatory burden. If you tried to open a nuclear power plant in New Hampshire right now, you would need to be in compliance with the entire massive list of regulations and fees outlined by the US 'Nuclear Regulatory Commission'[63] (NRC). Some of the dozens of annual fees cost millions[64] of dollars. But that isn't the hard part. You would need to read the entire chapter 1[65] of Title 10 of the Code of Federal Regulations. Considering that chapter 1 (nuclear energy regulations) has 199 parts, and each part contains around 35,000 words, it might literally take you a decade to read through all of the regulations. Keep in mind that the regulations carry the force of law. So, you would need to hire professionals to read it and to ensure that your plant complies with the many complicated regulations. These lawyers, compliance officers, and other experts might cost

you another few million or even billion dollars annually.

The same would be true for other types of power plants. Currently, it is not possible to open a natural gas or coal power plant unless you have the tremendous capital necessary to navigate the red tape created by DC over the past century. Among other agencies, these non-nuclear power plants are currently regulated by the federal government's Environmental Protection Agency (EPA). This agency also has essentially infinite regulations that no one person could possibly read, comprehend, and obey. It might require several decades for one person to read the whole Title 40[66] of the federal regulations, which is all of the EPA's laws. If you wish to comply with all of the EPA's rules, you may need to hire hundreds of well-trained lawyers, compliance officers, and other experts.

Even opening a new hydroelectric power plant would be an extremely difficult task if you lived in the united states. You would need to make sure that you comply with the regulations set by the Federal Energy Regulatory Commission[67] (FERC). Before considering opening such a plant, you should read Title 18[68] of the federal regulations and this 37-page document[69] regarding its rules. You may need to hire a few dozen lawyers, compliance officers, and other experts, and you'll probably need to keep them on your payroll permanently.

There are other forms of energy production that New Hampshire could pursue, especially if the federal government gets out of the way.

First designed in 1965, a 'molten salt reactor'[70] could produce large amounts of energy in an efficient, clean, and safe way. These facilities are small, modular, and do not need to be near a water source. They also use spent fuel that would otherwise go to waste, and they produce palladium as a byproduct, and no carbon dioxide. As explained by a member of the New Hampshire House 'Science, Technology & Energy Committee' and the 'NH Commission to Study Offshore Wind and Port Development':

"MSRs are small and modular...and they are very safe. If malfunction occurs, the molten salt hardens and contains any radiation spillage. MSR's do not need a water source like other nuclear technology and thus can be located anywhere, much closer to transmission lines, or provide micro-grids for towns and remote rural areas...MSR's use spent fuel that is otherwise being stored in hardened facilities at a very expensive cost to the taxpayers. We have enough spent fuel in NH to generate all of its electricity needs for more than 100 years. No mining needs to be done; the stuff is just sitting around in storage facilities...The spent fuel would not only be free, but the MSR owners might even be paid to remove the spent fuel from storage sites, getting rid of a very dangerous hazard that has thousands of years of half-life. This technology utilizes 97% of the remaining energy out of the spent fuel. It is super-efficient, unlike other nuclear technology. The resulting byproduct is valuable metals like palladium, which has a radiation half-life of about 50 years. It can be stored in a much less robust facility, and after 50 years, the precious metals are an asset that can be reclaimed."

Without the federal government's burdensome regulations, Granite Staters might find that opening their own nuclear power plant has become billions of dollars cheaper and years quicker. This decreased cost and increased supply of energy would dramatically reduce prices for the end consumer, which includes you and me. Add the tax savings (no more federal income taxes, federal business taxes, or any other federal taxes) into the equation, and the prospect of energy independence becomes a very simple one to understand for pro-independence New Hampshire residents.

It is certainly likely that once we cut ties to DC politicians and regulators, multiple power plants would open in New Hampshire very quickly.

While some naive detractors claim that it would be impossible for New Hampshire to receive energy from (newly) foreign nations, over $100 billion[71] of energy flows between Canada and the union annually. Energy currently flows freely between the states of the union and Canada. There is no reason to believe that any state would sever energy lines if the people of New Hampshire were to vote to govern themselves. New Hampshire's government would be very unlikely to do such a thing, because our legislators are sensible lawmakers and support free trade and free movement of all commodities, including energy. We acknowledge the reality that regardless of energy independence, a peak demand incident could cause us to require extra energy to satisfy our needs. Similarly, the legislators in other states and in DC would be very unlikely to sever energy ties with New Hampshire for two reasons. First, New Hampshire currently produces a substantial amount of energy, which could help other states when their demand peaks. Second, cutting ties to New Hampshire would harm those in Maine even more than those in New Hampshire.

Once New Hampshire is independent, Maine will be a non-contiguous state of the union (Like Alaska and Hawaii). If DC were to sever energy ties with New Hampshire, they would also be severing ties with Maine. If Maine chose to remain in the union, it would be forced to obey federal laws, regulations, and taxes, meaning that it would be in much worse shape than New Hampshire. The people of Maine might be forced to choose between freezing to death or seceding from the union. It is extremely unlikely that DC would make a major policy decision that would be terribly unpopular, harmful to American citizens, and encourage secession.

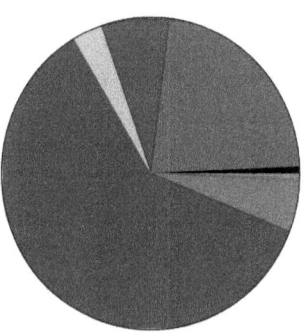

Sources of New Hampshire utility-scale electricity generation: full-year 2020[1]

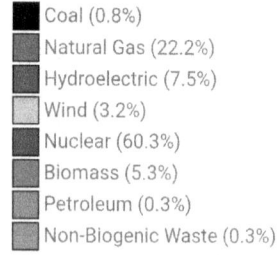

Coal (0.8%)
Natural Gas (22.2%)
Hydroelectric (7.5%)
Wind (3.2%)
Nuclear (60.3%)
Biomass (5.3%)
Petroleum (0.3%)
Non-Biogenic Waste (0.3%)

The Economy

How would our economy survive without being in the union?

Currently, New Hampshire seems to have the best economy of all 50 states in the union, judging by income, unemployment, and opportunity. The average income per resident in the live free or die state is 20% higher[72] than the union's average. The largest limiting factor is economic regulation, most of which comes from the federal government. Without infinite job-killing regulations coming from DC, New Hampshire's economy would likely soar to unprecedented heights.

Farmers and growers in New Hampshire produce a large amount of corn, potatoes, apples, maple syrup, dairy products, cattle, and hogs. New Hampshire's top industrial outputs are machinery, electric equipment, rubber, and plastic products. Hospitality and tourism are major components of the economy, as well. The state's largest economic sectors in 2018, based on contribution to GDP, are: 15% real estate and rental and leasing; 13% professional business services; 12% manufacturing; 10% government and government services; and 9% health care and social services.

The Seabrook Station Nuclear Power Plant is the largest nuclear reactor in New England and provides 57% of New Hampshire's electricity generation. Approximately 32% of New Hampshire's electricity consumption came from renewable resources (including nuclear, hydroelectric, wind, and other renewable resources). New Hampshire is a net exporter of electricity, exporting 63 trillion British thermal units (18 TWh).

According to a 2013 study by Phoenix Marketing International, New Hampshire had the 8th-highest percentage of millionaire households in the United States, at 6.48% of all households. In 2013, New Hampshire also had the lowest poverty rate in the union at just 8.7% of all residents, according to the Census Bureau.

Once we cut ties to DC politicians, the state's economy would explode into unprecedented prosperity for one large reason and for one massive reason. First, each worker would save around $30,000-50,000 per year once federal taxes no longer exist. These savings alone would more than make up for the 2-3 billion dollars sent from DC to the state government annually. The massive reason we'd prosper is regulation. Without DC politicians being our Lords and once we are no longer forced to obey the immeasurable number of federal laws and regulations, our businesses would be free to do what businesses do best: Create wealth. Currently, federal regulations cost American businesses **OVER 2 TRILLION**[73] dollars per year, according to a 2014 study. In 2022, regulations might cost businesses 3 or even 5 trillion dollars per year.

Considering that New Hampshire has 1.4 million people, this would amount to a savings of $10 billion for New Hampshire businesses annually. Considering the exponential nature of business growth, New Hampshire could be trillions richer within a few years.

One concern that I heard raised by a Liberty Block reader was whether commuters and federal contractors would need to find new jobs once New Hampshire separates from DC and begins to govern itself. This is a valid question.

Again, I cannot predict the future, as I have no idea what federal politicians would decide to do once New Hampshire severs ties with them. On the New Hampshire side of the issue, I cannot imagine a majority of our legislators supporting a wall, sanctions, or a prohibition against workers commuting to states in the union or working with federal contractors. Our legislature is very much pro-free-market and even more pro-travel and pro-immigration freedom. Likewise, I cannot imagine DC politicians (or legislatures of union states like Massachusetts) constructing a wall between them and New Hampshire or prohibiting the free movement and labor from our residents. They have been preaching the virtues of freedom of movement and condemning the concept of walls and movement restrictions for years. They could not possibly prevent people from moving across what they consider to be arbitrary and meaningless borders in order to earn a living.

However, in the likely-impossible worst case scenario of the DC politicians imposing a full on blockade of all trade in or out of New Hampshire (which itself is a literal act of war), we would still survive. We may not be the most prosperous nation in the world if we are forbidden from trading by the US military, but we would survive. As mentioned earlier, we have a relatively complete economy within our own borders. We have plenty of farms, animals, and other forms of food. We have lakes, rivers, and oceans for fishing. We have many large forests and plenty of animals. We produce many critical materials and we have a tremendous technology sector, which is increasingly important in today's world. We would be just fine.

Even if the US military sent all of their soldiers to our borders to block interstate trade, they could not totally stop us from earning money from others around the world. Granite Staters could still sell all sorts of virtual products and services (classes, virtual assistants, advertising, consulting, editing, video, music, etc.) to people all over the world as long as they have internet access. And those people could pay the Granite Staters in crypto-currency, which the government cannot stop without shutting down the world's internet. There is nothing DC politicians would be able to do about our internet-based economic prosperity. Considering that New Hampshire is one of the crypto-currency and technology capitals of the world, this bodes very well for an independent nation.

We addressed the issue of currency and interstate travel in previous chapters.

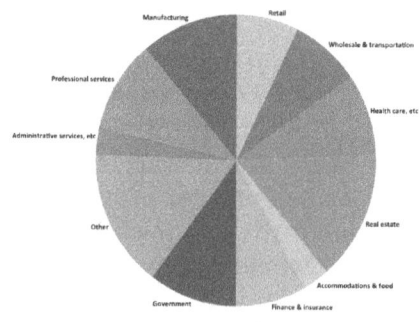

Source: Bureau of Economic Analysis.

Education

Once New Hampshire leaves the union, what would our education system look like? Would it collapse without federal funding and support? Would our students suffer? Would we still be able to transfer seamlessly between colleges in other states of the union?

These are valid questions.

Let's begin by taking a quick look at the education system within New Hampshire:

As of 2021, there were 185,000 students[74] from pre-k through high school. Around 4,000 students[75] were home-schooled. There were also 189,000[76] college students attending the 25 colleges within the state.

The New Hampshire government spends over $2.6 billion[77] per year on education. The state government's annual budget[78] is $6.5 billion, and municipalities add their own taxation and spending for education. The state's education trust fund is funded by various sources, including $100 million[79] from the NH lottery system, $300 million from taxes on businesses, and $360 million from property taxes. In addition to state funding, municipalities raise $2 billion from the local portion of property taxes and use the money to fund their government-run school systems on a local level.

The federal government takes around $4 trillion dollars by force from citizens throughout the united states annually. Each year, politicians from DC send around $2 billion[80] to the New Hampshire government, much of which is comprised of education grants.

When DC sends money back to New Hampshire in the form of education grants, they require that all of the schools in the government school system obey extra restrictions. This is in addition to all federal laws in Title 34[81] of the Federal Code, which would take a lifetime to read in its entirety. A well-known example of the federal government using extortion to convince state governments to obey their commands involved the 'Common Core'[82] standards for English language arts and mathematics. As of this writing, New Hampshire and nearly every other state has accepted the 'Common Core' federal standards[83] because they wanted the federal money.

Of course, all of the money sent from DC politicians to states and localities for education spending was obtained by taxing workers throughout the union.

Years after its implementation, progressive states like New York[84] still cannot even educate half of their public school students to a 'proficient' level in Math or English language arts (the two categories they measure) according to their own data. After leaving their government-run high school, only one in four students in NYC is deemed 'college ready', as reported by PublicSchoolReview.com[85]. Throughout the united states, government spending[86] on education has skyrocketed while actual educational achievement has remained flat or worsened.

Without federal influence, New Hampshire's students would be much more likely to receive the education that their parents and other policymakers in New Hampshire decide is best for them. If you believe that DC politicians know how to best educate your children, you should not support independence. If you believe that New Hampshire's parents could and should be the primary decision makers in the education of their children, you should support independence.

Practically speaking, independence from DC politicians is unlikely to stop the constant flow of students across the state's borders in both directions. Many students would likely still travel from southern New Hampshire to study in Boston and elsewhere, and many students from Massachusetts, Maine, Vermont, and elsewhere would still study in New Hampshire's colleges.

If a person believed that this would not be the case, they would be claiming that the anti-border, pro-travel federal government suddenly would lock down its northern border and prohibit travel to or from the union. This is extremely unlikely and would be among the most hypocritical policy changes by a government in world history. The federal government (both major parties) have been increasingly supportive of totally eliminating all of their borders for the past few decades. And we know that New Hampshire's legislature certainly would not close its borders, either.

Regardless of travel to and from the state, New Hampshire's students could continue to excel in all aspects of their education, including college and graduate school. Within our state, we have 25 colleges, a medical school, a law school, and various other graduate programs. This means that even if our students could not leave the state for some reason, we would be just fine, and we could still produce plenty of doctors and lawyers.

Perhaps the most drastic change that would occur if New Hampshire declared independence from the union would be the tremendous prosperity of education faculty and support workers. Currently, teachers and other school employees in New Hampshire pay around 20-30% of their income to DC politicians under the threat of force. Once we cut ties with the federal government, all of that money would stay in their pockets. If you want to give every teacher in the state a 33% raise, you should consider supporting independence.

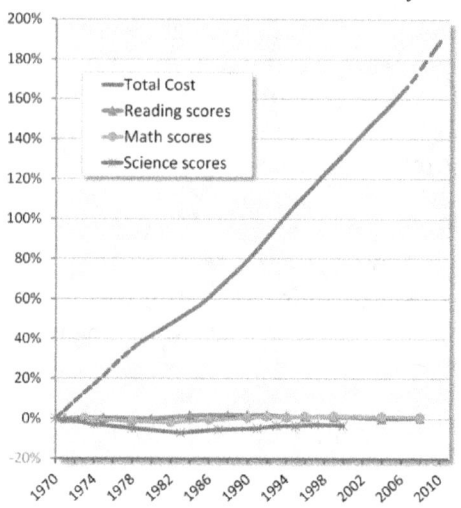

Trends in inflation-adjusted total cost of a K-through-12 public education and achievement of 17-year-olds (U.S.)

Cato Institute

"Total cost" is the whole amount spent on the K-12 education of a student graduating in the given year. We graph the percent change in that amount--and in test scores--over time.

Data sources
(test scores): NAEP, *Long Term Trends* reports, U.S. Department of Education (cost): *Digest of Education Statistics 2011*, Table 191, U.S. DOE, CPI adjusted to constant 2012 $. Missing values linearly interpolated or extrapolated.

Prepared Sept. 2012 by:
Andrew J. Coulson, Director, Cato Institute Center for Educational Freedom

Federal Land

The DC politicians do claim ownership of the land in a multitude of places in New Hampshire. This does make separation from the union challenging, though certainly not impossible. As with nearly any divorce, determining how to divide property is one of the most complicated and controversial matters.

The White Mountain National Forest
A large area in the middle of the state is owned by those in DC and is controlled by the Forest Service, a division of the US Dept. of Agriculture[87]. The land mass spans 1,225 square miles, though 5.65% of it resides in Maine. The simplest course of action would be for New Hampshire to take ownership of the part of the forest that lies within its borders. Many believe that this would entail a transfer of money from New Hampshire to DC. This may be the case, though the matter is extremely complicated considering federal debt, the current status of shared ownership and custodianship, park revenue, and potentially dozens more factors. In the worst case scenario, New Hampshire would compensate the federal government for the land. This payment would likely not cause any trouble for New Hampshire due to its tremendous wealth and prosperity, as explained in earlier chapters. The same concepts apply to the Great Bay National Wildlife Refuge[88] and any other land within New Hampshire that the DC politicians have taken over throughout the past decades, in a process that some compare to theft[89]. These areas could be used to generate substantial revenue for the government by using it creatively, as well.

Fortunately, the DC politicians have only stolen 14%[90] of New Hampshire's land. The feds claim ownership of 28% of the land throughout the united states, including 98.5% of Alaska, 80% of Nevada, and over 60% of Utah and Idaho. In 2016, Obama stole millions of acres[91] from Nevada and Utah, with the stroke of a pen. In total, Obama took over 265 million acres[92] of land and water, more than any other president.

Federal prison
There is one federal prison in New Hampshire, and it only houses 587 inmates. The chapter about law enforcement explains how simple it would be to transfer these prisoners to another federal prison, which happens regularly. The prisoners could also be transferred to the New Hampshire state prison. They could also be released. There are at least three viable and reasonable options.

Courts
There is only one federal court in New Hampshire. It is called the 'United States District Court for the District of New Hampshire'. There are only three judges on this court. Once New Hampshire is independent, the judges can very easily be transferred to another district court, promoted to a circuit court in the federal system, retire, or find a new job. Two of the three judges graduated from law school over 30 years ago, meaning that they can likely retire quite easily by the time New Hampshire secedes, a process which will likely not be completed for at least two years from this writing. The federal courthouse in Concord could be transferred to the New Hampshire state government. Ideally, it could be purchased back from the DC Empire for the same

price they paid for it when they seized it, which I suspect was roughly zero dollars.

Post offices

The federal government currently operates 235 post offices[93] within New Hampshire. During the secession negotiation, these small offices will likely be transferred back to the state or local government, or auctioned off to the public. I would even support a law allowing the DC Empire to keep the revenue from the auctions, especially if it would help make the divorce easier for them to swallow. If the DC politicians choose to sell the offices back to the state, they should expect the legislature to pay them what they paid when they first took the offices. As for the mail service itself, New Hampshire would likely no longer operate within the US Postal Service system. Naturally, spontaneous order would ensure that multiple mailing services would compete for your service (FedEx, UPS, and others already do, and Amazon could probably set up an efficient system in a matter of weeks). This would likely lead to people being able to send anything in the mail to any part of the world with the courier service of their choosing. If they didn't like the service, they would choose another private company. If all companies were terrible, I and other entrepreneurs would create our own mail service. Keep in mind that this federal agency loses over $9 billion per year[94] and is plagued by corruption[95] and many other issues[96]. To say that the department is inefficient would be a ridiculous understatement. There is no doubt that private companies could (and do) perform much better than the feds.

Pease Air Force Base
This former US Air Force base was closed down[97] by the federal government in 1989. In 1990, the NH legislature drafted a law creating the Pease Development Authority (PDA), granting the PDA the power to implement the base redevelopment plan with the 3,000 acre lot.

In 1991, Pease opened for civilian use through an Airfield Joint Use Agreement (AJUA) with the United States Air Force, with a field-base operator offering services to general aviation. Zoning was adopted to provide for four different types of development: a 797-acre airport zone, a 448-acre airport industrial zone, a 333-acre industrial zone, and a 466-acre business/commercial zone. Additionally, 781 acres were set aside for natural resource protection and wetlands mitigation. In 1993, Businesses began coming to Pease, including Lonza Biologics, Red Hook Brewery and Two International Group.

It is difficult to ascertain exactly who owns Pease. It seems to be run by a board of directors and by the government of New Hampshire. It probably should not be considered federal land, though the federal government is permitted to use the airfield. Occam's Razor would say that the federal government would continue to enjoy access to this strategic location which its airplanes could utilize after New Hampshire leaves the union. The USAF already has air force bases[98] in Germany, Qatar, Italy, Japan, Korea, Spain, Turkey, Britain, and possibly in other countries. If the feds could access a base in New Hampshire, it would not exactly be a radical idea.

Regardless of the type of federal land, the comprehensive negotiations that are sure to occur as

New Hampshire peacefully separates from the union will iron out the details of which properties go to each party. The difficulties presented by the DC Empire annexing land throughout New Hampshire over the past few decades is unlikely to be the biggest challenge related to independence. Recall that the federal politicians have stolen 14% of our land. Interestingly, New Hampshire law prohibits the federal government[99] from owning more than 2% of our land. Of course, the feds have no respect for any laws that limit their authority. Maybe that's one of the many reasons secession has become so popular.

Just how popular is New Hampshire independence?

Public Support For Independence

How do the people of New Hampshire feel about secession? Do they really want to be independent from the federal government? Would they even support placing the question on the ballot?

A June 2022 poll by SurveyUSA[100] asked New Hampshire residents how they felt about the federal government and the idea of separating from the union. Among the most interesting questions were:

Elected leaders in the federal government have my best interests in mind when passing legislation: Agree or disagree?

Only 4% strongly agree, only 25% somewhat agree, and 66% disagree.

Politicians in Washington, DC violate our rights more than they protect our rights. Agree or disagree?

22% strongly agree, 43% somewhat agree, and only 27% disagree.

(Considering that the sole reason for the establishment of the federal government was to protect natural rights, shouldn't this mean that it should not exist - because it violates the rights it was designed to protect?)

People in the united states are growing more divided over important issues, such as LGBT rights, guns, abortion, election integrity, race relations, involvement in foreign wars, climate change, immigration, etc. Agree or disagree?

60% strongly agree, 31% somewhat agree, and only 6% disagree.

If the citizens of the united states continue to get more divided on major issues, I fear that political violence will increase. Agree or disagree?

89% agree and only 7% disagree.

I trust my state government more than I trust the federal government. Agree or disagree?

63% agree and only 24% disagree.

The survey also found that 29% of New Hampshire residents and 52% of New Hampshire Republicans said they were ready to secede. The survey also answered the common question about the DC Empire deploying their military to attack any state that chose to secede. When asked if the federal government should use military force in response to a state seceding, only 3% of New Hampshire residents and 6% of the respondents throughout the union supported the idea. In regard to how passionately New Hampshire feels about independence, only 65% of respondents said that they would not donate to the campaign for independence. Only 59% of respondents said that they would not volunteer for the campaign for independence. How confident and passionate are the anti-independence folks in New Hampshire? Not confident enough to have a public debate on the issue.

Throughout the union, polling consistently shows that around 75% of people believe the union is heading in the wrong direction and that there must be a drastic change to our current arrangement. As of this writing, only 13% of people think that we are on the right track, according to a massive survey[101] by Civiqs.com. A July 2022 poll[102] conducted by Yahoo/YouGov found that only 15% of people think that we are on the right track as a union. The same poll found that only 43% of respondents said they'd be worse off if their states left the union and became independent nations.

Increasingly, people throughout New Hampshire are giving up on 'saving DC' and are supporting independence as the last hope for the future of liberty. Within a decade, these people will likely comprise the majority in the live free or die state.

Constitutionality

Is secession constitutional? Does it matter? After all, secession from the larger government, union, or empire is rarely considered 'legal' by the larger government. In 1776, it was certainly illegal for the colonists to violently rebel and secede from Great Britain, at least if you ask the British government. That secession was violent, whereas modern New Hampshire secession would be peaceful. That secession involved colonists rebelling against their own king, whereas modern New Hampshire secession would involve a state exiting a union that it joined under a contract which has been thoroughly violated.

The legislation that would allow New Hampshire voters to cast a ballot in favor of independence has been assigned to the House Federal-State Relations Committee. One member of that committee has sent a frantic letter to his colleagues begging them to oppose the legislation and prevent the people from having a chance to vote on whether to become a self-governing state no longer bound to DC politicians. Rep. Brodie Deshaies sent the same letter to me when I asked him to support CACR32. I asked him multiple times if he or any other opponent of independence would be willing to debate me, and he has declined to answer, each time repeating that his issues are addressed in this letter and that he will not debate me. His letter is below, with my commentary in italics.

Why NH Secession is Impossible
In this upcoming legislative session, every NH State Representative will be voting on a constitutional amendment—CACR32—that purports to make NH a

"sovereign nation." And I use the word "purports" very explicitly—you will read why later.

This means NH State Legislators will vote on articles of secession. I am amazed any lawmaker should have to pen a letter on this issue. Nonetheless, someone must explain why articles of secession are reckless and impossible.

Technically, legislators are voting on whether to allow NH voters to vote on articles of secession, so this is not necessarily totally accurate.

Part I: Catastrophic Consequences
Let's look at the logistics first. Thirty-two percent of NH's total revenue comes from the federal government. This revenue pays for infrastructure, social security, Medicare, Medicaid, and other essential services for our state's residents. If NH lost all of this revenue, we would immediately need to increase all business taxes and establish sales and income taxes. Even if we stopped offering most of these services, the cost of infrastructure alone would be insurmountable. Secession would kill the NH Advantage.

This is a very common myth, and the opposite is true. Right now, New Hampshire workers send DC billions of dollars via federal income taxes, corporate taxes, and other taxes. Only 3 billion is sent back to NH, and DC politicians place conditions on each of those dollars. Once independent from DC, the average NH worker may save around $20-50k per year because federal taxes would no longer exist. Perhaps equally important, all federal regulations - which cost the American economy over $2 trillion per year - would no longer exist in NH. This would also cause the NH economy to boom like no *economy ever in human history. Taken together, the radical decrease in taxes and regulations would cause our economy to become the most prosperous one in the world by incredible amounts. Keep in mind that NH already has the highest median household income in the union.*

Secession would have a terrible impact on state collected revenue. The state collects thirty-four percent of its revenue from business taxes and another twelve percent from Meals and Rooms Taxes, also known as our rentals tax. These two state taxes overwhelmingly make up our revenue stream and would be impacted if we left the Union. We would no longer have free trade within the world's largest consumer market. Our economy and state revenues would tank, forcing us to adopt sales and income taxes and kill the NH Advantage again.

Few (if any) legislators or residents in New Hampshire would wish to cut off shoppers, visitors, and businesses from crossing our state border. Interstate trade would actually continue much like it does today. Would DC politicians embargo New Hampshire? I can't speak for them, but embargo is an act of war[103] and would unnecessarily punish millions of people in New Hampshire and the rest of the union, not to mention cutting off Maine from the union entirely. If you believe that DC politicians would declare war against us for leaving....that is all the more reason we SHOULD leave them!

Other nations would not recognize NH as a "sovereign nation." We would become a destitute hermit republic. No one would be able to travel to our state—killing tourism, our largest industry—and we would lack the funds and infrastructure to protect our borders. NH would be alone and vulnerable in a globalizing world.

Again, what is this paranoid assumption based on? Over the past 80 years, 150 small nations separated from their countries/unions and nearly every single one was recognized by the international community. That said, nobody argues that the most corrupt, evil, authoritarian regimes may not recognize legitimate countries. Despite Taiwan being a totally unique and independent island nation, politicians who run China refuse to recognize Taiwan as an independent nation. Only 14 tiny UN-recognized states recognize Taiwan as an independent state. Yet, the Taiwanese remain prosperous, patriotic, and safe (the only threat to Taiwanese people is the Chinese politicians). In 2021, Bloomberg Media actually named Taiwan as the #1 place in the world[104] for Americans to live. The average income in Taiwan of $16,355[105] blows China's average of $4,246 out of the water. If not for government gangs, free trade would obviously allow the Taiwanese and all other humans on Earth to be exponentially more prosperous.

Not to mention that federal officials with the backing of the US military, the most well-funded and prepared military in the world, would never allow NH to secede. Every NH Guardsman swears an oath to the US and NH Constitutions. They are bound to protect the "perpetual Union" our US Constitution establishes. This is part of the principle of "dual enlistment," under which persons enlisted in state militias (National Guard) units simultaneously enlist in the National Guard of the United States. And when National Guard units are called to active duty in the federal service, Guardsmen are relieved of their status in the state militia. The NH National Guard would immediately help federal troops reestablish control over any purportedly "sovereign" NH.

I already alluded to this earlier, but if your best argument against leaving an abusive partner is that 'if you try to leave, he will kill you, then you have a terrible argument. If I were advising my friend to leave her husband, the fact that her husband is so violent that he might kill her if she tried leaving would only give me more *reason to advise her to leave, not more reason to stay. But he mentions the sacred 'Constitution' here, so let's address it. To directly quote Representative Deshaies, "Every NH Guardsman swears an oath to the US and NH Constitutions." Okay, if the Constitution is so important, and if they are really determined to obey it religiously, they would have arrested every member of Congress who supported any violation of the Constitution. Of course, nearly every single member of Congress (not to mention every president, judge, and federal agent) supports at least some form of gun control, as well as violations of the 1st, 4th, 5th, 9th, and 10th amendments. Once US soldiers begin arresting everyone in DC for violating the Constitution, I'll start taking this argument seriously.*

Now, regarding the NH Constitution, let's take a look at what it says about rebellion:

"[Art.] 10. [Right of Revolution.] Government being instituted for the common benefit, protection, and security, of the whole community, and not for the private interest or emolument of any one man, family, or class of men; therefore, whenever the ends of

government are perverted, and public liberty manifestly endangered, and all other means of redress are ineffectual, the people may, and of right ought to reform the old, or establish a new government. The doctrine of nonresistance against arbitrary power, and oppression, is absurd, slavish, and destructive of the good and happiness of mankind. - June 2, 1784"

Part II: Unquestionably Unconstitutional

NH could never survive as a "sovereign nation." You may say to yourself, "out of principle, we should still leave the Union and see what happens." But articles of secession are unconstitutional and therefore impossible. Any attempt to make NH a "sovereign nation" only purports to do so and is illegitimate.

The first legal argument why states cannot secede from the Union is reasonably understandable. The federal government is the only legitimate power to admit new states and extend or retract territorial boundaries. Nowhere in our US Constitution does it allow the federal government to permit any state to secede, let alone for any state to decide unilaterally. Our Constitution is quite clear on this issue (see Article IV, Section 3). No state constitution has ever suggested that states hold this power. Constitutions are implicit contracts with citizens that grant governments specific powers. With no power explicitly given allowing secession, no state can ever secede.

I don't think the Representative is making the argument he thinks he's making here. The question is whether the people of New Hampshire have the right to self-governance. First, the state entered the union 240 years ago, meaning that nobody currently alive in New Hampshire has ever had an opportunity to make their voice heard or to cast a vote on whether they'd like to remain under the thumb of DC politicians. Second, the reader must understand that 'state has always been synonymous with 'country'. Indeed, New Hampshire went from being a British Colony to a self-governing state in 1776. Later, a few delegates from New Hampshire agreed to be part of an alliance in a union with the other former colonies, represented by an extremely weak central government. They thought that the central government would obey the Constitution, and would only serve to settle interstate commerce disputes and organize the military. Obviously, they were very wrong, and that weak central government has grown into one of the most authoritarian regimes in world history, and it continues to grow at breakneck speed, taxing and abusing every individual in the united states increasingly each day. But here's the important thing: The 10th amendment to the US Constitution is very clear, and it says the exact opposite of what Deshaies claims: **"The powers not delegated to the United States by the Constitution, nor prohibited by it to the states, are reserved to the states respectively, or to the people."** And the Constitution does not delegate to the federal government the power to prevent any state from leaving the union. This means that the right to secession IS allowed by the US Constitution. I am not sure why he mentions Article IV section 3, which clearly says nothing about secession: "New States may be admitted by the Congress into this Union; but no new State shall be formed or erected within the Jurisdiction of any other State; nor any State be formed by the Junction of two or more States, or Parts of States, without the Consent of the Legislatures of the States concerned as well as of the Congress."

Furthermore, Article 1, Section 10 of the US Constitution clearly lists everything that states may not do. Guess which action didn't make the list? Secession.

Another argument lies in the US Supreme Court's decision *Texas v. White* (1869). In the court's majority decision, Chief Justice Salmon P. Chase explained that the Union began during the Revolutionary War amongst the colonies. In his decision, he writes, the Union "was confirmed and strengthened... and received definite form and character and sanction from the Articles of Confederation... [and] by these, the Union was solemnly declared to 'be perpetual.'" Justice Chase then says that our current Constitution was "ordained 'to form a more perfect Union,'" which intended to "convey the idea of indissoluble unity...." Therefore, the Union can never be dissolved. Our form of government and Constitution is predicated upon the Union's "'perpetual'" existence. Without this "'perpetual'" existence, we would be throwing away the Union, and with it, the US Constitution.

Okay, now we are getting to the heart of his argument. He believes that the judges who sit in DC are Gods who can interpret the US Constitution however they desire. A politician in a long black robe in DC does not get to rewrite the Constitution, nor does he have the magical power to override the natural right to self-governance or to freedom in general. I wish that somebody would ask Deshaies whether he would faithfully obey the court's ruling as canon if they determined that no individuals in the united states may possess a firearm, because it violated the 'general welfare' clause of the US Constitution. Simply put, I and the others in New

Hampshire don't care what elites in DC say. Just like the founders who we all claim to respect didn't care what the king said. The king made it clear that rebellion was treason; but the founders still did so, and every American now celebrates their victory every 4th of July. Nobody even argued that it was legal to secede from Britain. They all knew that the government of Britain considered it a crime to leave. That was kind of the whole point of leaving; to get away from tyrants.

If the Constitution was a contract (it's not), then it would have been voided long ago when the government violated it. In contract law, the most foundational premise is that if one party willfully violates the contract, the other party could choose to break the contract off. And the federal government has violated the Constitution countless times and continues to increasingly violate it. If we are discussing the constitutionality of things, then I would argue that according to the Constitution, the US government should no longer exist.

The last Constitutional argument is straightforward. It does not matter whether or not secession is illegal. What matters is that the Union beat the Confederacy in the Civil War. Once this happened, the illegality of unilateral secession was *de facto* established. The legality of secession was answered at Appomattox Court House in 1865 with the conclusion of the Civil War. It also means the repercussions for attempting unilateral secession have been decided too. The federal government must punish states and their leaders who try to secede.

*Ah, one of my favorite arguments against state independence: **Might makes right!** "Sweetheart, your husband may beat the hell out of you, starve you, and abuse you in every which way, but the legality of divorce or separation was settled when he beat you into a coma last time you tried to leave him. So, you will just need to stay with him forever. Might makes right. He is stronger than you. Therefore, he is right and you are wrong.", he advises his female friend after she cries to him about her abusive husband.*

Which leads us to another question: Can state leaders introduce or vote for articles of secession? No. They cannot, and that is not my opinion. It is what our Constitution explicitly states. The 14th Amendment, Article III, is very clear. No State Legislator shall engage in rebellion against the Constitution. Voting for NH's proposed articles of secession is rebellion against the US Constitution. It would be casting a vote to rebel against the Union and, therefore, the same Constitution establishing the perpetual Union.

Again, the Constitutional arguments are perhaps the weakest arguments against independence. To be honest, if the DC government gang obeyed the Constitution, the massive amount of discontent among Americans and the New Hampshire independence movement would not exist. So, if DC politicians can brazenly violate the US Constitution ad infinitum, I am totally fine doing the same, even if it leads them to accuse me of breaking their laws. Again, that would put me in the company of George Washington and Thomas Jefferson. I'm okay with that. If you do like Constitutions, you should read this part of the New Hampshire Constitution, which literally legalizes and encourages rebellion against tyrannical government, such as we have now in DC: "...whenever the ends of government are perverted, and public liberty manifestly endangered, and all other means of redress are ineffectual, the people may, and of right ought to reform the old, or establish a new government. The doctrine of nonresistance against arbitrary power, and oppression, is absurd, slavish, and destructive of the good and happiness of mankind."

State lawmakers have also introduced legislation establishing a process to remove members of the General Court who have "engaged in insurrection or rebellion." HB1007 would allow the NH House or Senate to enforce Section III of the 14th Amendment. Article VI, Paragraph 2 of the US Constitution—commonly referred to as the Supremacy Clause—establishes the federal constitution and federal law as taking precedence over state laws and even state constitutions. State lawmakers must abide by our US Constitution. Therefore, I would conclude that we are duty-bound to fulfill Section III of the 14th Amendment.

Another anti-freedom, anti-independence legislator proposed an unconstitutional bill[106] to remove pro-independence patriots from the legislature. The bill won't pass and is not even worth spending time worrying about.

I encourage fellow lawmakers to reject NH's articles of secession and protect constitutional government. Not only is CACR32 logistically and constitutionally impossible, but NH's articles of secession may require enforcement of the 14th Amendment. The NH House should not be forcing America into a constitutional crisis. The question of unilateral state secession died in Appomattox. Let's keep it that way.

I encourage all lawmakers to support the natural right to self-governance, reject paranoid propaganda, and protect ourselves from the tyrants in DC. And reject the notion that might makes right. Help us protect the smallest minority: the individual. Please allow the people of New Hampshire to vote on whether they want our great state to continue to suffer under the vicious rule of corrupt DC politicians, judges, law enforcement agents, and regulators.

In summary, there is nothing in the NH or US Constitution that prohibits secession. And very few people would disagree with the fact that anything not prohibited by the US Constitution is certainly legal. Even if the US Constitution were a contract (which is the best argument that anti-independence loyalists present) we could simply point to the countless examples over the past century of the federal government violating the Constitution/contract with increasing severity. And we know that the most fundamental tenet of contract law is severability; the concept that if one party violates the contract with willful intent and does not immediately correct the violation, the other party is totally within its rights to void the entire contract. In the simplest terms, once the federal government passed the massive 'National Firearms Act' which clearly violated the Constitution's 2nd amendment protection of the right to keep and bear arms without infringement, any state could have walked away from the union with good reason, according to universal contract law.

After this book was originally published, an anti-independence citizen filed a complaint against the legislators who voted to place independence on the ballot. Karen Steele asked the New Hampshire Ballot Law Commission to block 13 State Representatives from appearing on the ballot for reelection in the 2022 elections. She claimed that the 14th amendment to the US Constitution prohibits legislators who engage in *'insurrection or rebellion'* from holding office. The Ballot Law Commission consists of five members, the Secretary of State, and the Attorney General. The five members are appointed by the Speaker of the House, the Senate President, the Governor, and the Executive Council. At this particular meeting, the Secretary of State was present and the assistant Attorney General was present.The assistant AG explained that there is no reasonable way to come to the conclusion that the pro-independence legislators engaged in any form of 'insurrection or rebellion', because such acts are necessarily violent. It is not disputed that the pro-independence legislators are entirely peaceful and non-violent. In fact, the proposed amendment literally called for peaceful separation from the DC tyrants:

[Art.] 7-a. [Independent Nation.] New Hampshire peaceably declares independence from the United States and immediately proceeds as a sovereign nation. All other references to the United States in this constitution, state statutes, and regulations are nullified."

Courageous legislators who support allowing NH voters to have an opportunity to vote on independence

The hearing ended with the BLC voting unanimously[107] to dismiss the ridiculous complaint.

Part 2, Article 20 of the New Hampshire Constitution provides that the House of Representatives *"shall be judge of the returns, elections, and qualifications, of its members, as pointed out in this Constitution."* The Complaint alleges that all of the persons for whom disqualification is sought are currently members of the New Hampshire House of Representatives. Yet, no action has been taken by that body to disqualify those members for their actions. According to the Constitution, the Ballot Law Commission has no authority to make such a determination in the absence of a determination by the House of Representatives to that effect.

Up until this point, we were on defense (though our opponents were afraid to debate us publicly). We easily stopped their attack at the BLC. I later wrote an article toying with the idea of going on offense against the unethical anti-independence legislators like Deshaies and Smith:

On March 10th, the New Hampshire House of Representatives killed the legislation[108] that sought to allow the voters to determine whether the State should remain in the union. Since the public hearing for CACR32 in January, many citizens have been asking the legislature to allow them to vote on an important question on which the people have not had any input since the illegitimate constitution[109] was controversially ratified by a few politicians some 245 years ago.

The anti-liberty legislators knew that independence had a large amount of support among people and legislators. So, they utilized all the tools at their disposal to ensure that no legislators could vote in favor of the legislation, even if some of those methods were legally questionable.

According to Article 30 of the New Hampshire Constitution:

"[Art.] 30. [Freedom of Speech.] The freedom of deliberation, speech, and debate, in either House of the Legislature, is so essential to the rights of the people, that it cannot be the foundation of any action, complaint, or prosecution, in any other Court or place whatsoever."

The New Hampshire Constitution – the highest law of our State is clear: legislators enjoy complete freedom of speech to propose and support any legislation they desire, and in regards to their capacities as legislators, they can never be punished for their speech, no matter what, especially if it is totally peaceful.

If it were a crime to propose legislation such as CACR32, there is no way that the Office of Legislative Services would have published it, and it is unlikely that the Attorney General would have allowed the legislation to proceed without arresting and charging the sponsors. Additionally, Sununu, the Secretary of State, and other officials would not have remained silent for months since the bill was introduced.

The legislators who oppose independence and consider themselves the brightest minds in the universe surely are familiar with this Article of our Constitution. Yet, they seemingly violated it numerous times over the past few months by accusing supporters of CACR32 with treason, rebellion, and insurrection. They even went so far as to threaten to kick them out of the legislature or prosecute them for treason. This legally questionable tactic had a massive effect on the trajectory of the bill. In the House Committee on State-Federal Relations, at least two representatives who had said that they would vote in favor of the bill changed their positions, following the assertions of Rep. Deshaies linking support of this CACR to insurrection, rebellion and treason.

Could Deshaies and others be prosecuted for violating the NH Constitution by threatening members in order to influence their votes?

During the public hearing in January, the committee chairman allowed Deshaies to speak for 27 minutes, an unusually long duration. During his speech, Deshaies argued that this legislation was tantamount to rebellion and insinuated that DC politicians could and should send the military to NH to kill those who support the legislation.

Under State law, one could argue that this would be considered criminal threatening, as well. New Hampshire Title LXII Section 631:4[110] states that a person is guilty of criminal threatening when *"The person threatens to commit any crime against the property of another with a purpose to coerce or terrorize any person."* Interestingly, the term 'terrorism' generally includes the threat of force to coerce a person to do something, especially for political gain. In this case, one might argue that Deshaies could be charged with criminal threatening against the seven sponsors of CACR32 when he said during the hearing that *"Every vote cast [by Representatives] is aiding...every vote for it has constitutional ramifications judging by amendment 14:3 of the US Constitution. Some scholars would argue that this is rebellion. This very well could be an argument that voting for this....aiding and abetting in that process could very arguably be unconstitutional..."*

He also said that the federal government would kill those who seek to peacefully leave their union, and he implied that he would support such a decision.

Interestingly, Deshaies also said in the hearing that *"It's great that we're entering into a constitutional process...The members who proposed this....it's their right."* This statement seems contradictory.

"Screw personal liberty and screw the NH Constitution! Anyone who wants to let the voters decide whether to oppose DC politicians is guilty of treason against our Lords in DC!"

Lastly, the anti-independence legislators may have violated House rules at Thursday's session. The rules[111] that the legislators agreed upon states in section 1:4 that *"Legislators shall treat each other, legislative employees, and the public with dignity and respect."* Of course, one could argue that threatening to remove a member from the legislature and threatening to imprison them is disrespectful and undignified, especially when taking into account the strong protection that legislators' speech has within the House chamber.

During his floor speech[112], Representative Tim Smith (D-Manchester) may have also violated the NH Constitution, State law, and House rules when he said that *"It was really close to the textbook definition under title 18 of USC... of advocating overthrow of the US government when this CACR was introduced. When cosponsors signed on, it was really close to seditious conspiracy. A vote for this is really close to the federal definition of treason!"*

Will there be investigations and potential charges filed against these statists? Will they be disciplined by the state government?

The End

Further reading

The Plague That Must Not Be Questioned – Elliot "Alu" Axelman
Presumed Guilty – Elliot "Alu" Axelman
They Fear Unity – Elliot "Alu" Axelman
Taxation Is Theft – Elliot "Alu" Axelman
The Blueprint For Liberty – Elliot "Alu" Axelman
How Amazing Is The US Constitution? – Elliot "Alu" Axelman
The Progressive Solution – Elliot "Alu" Axelman & Marcus Evans
1984 – George Orwell
The Myth of the Rational Voter – Bryan Caplan
Dumbing Us Down – John Taylor Gatto
The Fountainhead – Ayn Rand
Government: The biggest Scam In History – Howard Lichtman
Follow The Money – Dan Bongino
Pandemia – Alex Berenson
Shadow Bosses – Mallory Factor
The Creature From Jekyll Island – G. Edward Griffin
Work For Liberty – Conner Drigotas
End The Fed – Ron Paul
The Case Against Education – Bryan Caplan
Animal Farm – George Orwell
The Moral Case For Fossil Fuels – Alex Epstein
Human Action – Ludwig Von Mises
Atlas Shrugged – Ayn Rand
Fahrenheit 451 – Ray Bradbury
Man, Economy, & State – Murray Rothbard
Basic Economics – Thomas Sowell
Wealth of Nations – Adam Smith
The Law – Frédéric Bastiat
Economics In One Lesson – Henry Hazlitt
Rich Dad Poor Dad – Robert Kiyosaki
Faucian Bargain – Steve Deace & Todd Erzen
Blue Dawn – Blaine Pardoe
Texit – Daniel Miller
Secret Empires – Peter Schweizer

Thank you very much for reading this pamphlet. If you have any questions about New Hampshire independence that were not answered, please reach out to NHindependence.org, LibertyBlock.com, or email alu.axelman@gmail.com.

If you enjoyed this book, please leave a review on Amazon. The QR code leading to the page is below.

Any tip would be greatly appreciated!

Endnotes

1. https://amzn.to/3we4m9W
2. https://www.heritage.org/health-care-reform/report/obamacare-and-the-individual-mandate-violating-personal-liberty-and
3. https://sgp.fas.org/crs/misc/R45146.pdf
4. https://www.wsj.com/articles/SB10001424052702304319804576389601079728920
5. https://www.crbgroup.com/insights/pharmaceuticals/drug-approval-process
6. https://freedomfirstnetwork.com/2021/09/a-legacy-of-corruption-in-the-fda-and-big-pharma
7. https://libertyblock.com/a-manchin-of-corruption/
8. https://www.healthcaredive.com/news/scotus-narrowly-upholds-health-worker-vaccine-mandate/617000/
9. https://taxprof.typepad.com/taxprof_blog/2012/05/all-hospitals.html
10. https://libertyblock.com/4-reasons-payroll-tax-is-worse-than-income-tax/
11. https://libertyblock.com/a-bipartisan-transplant-bill-new-hampshires-people-can-live-with/
12. https://surgerycenterok.com/
13. https://original.antiwar.com/eland/2015/10/26/endless-war-makes-us-less-safe/
14. https://www.yahoo.com/entertainment/news/ny-times-hillary-clinton-approved-russian-uranium-deal-133318767.html?
15. https://nypost.com/2021/08/20/us-left-billions-in-weapons-in-afghanistan-with-black-hawks-in-talibans-hands/
16. https://www.huffpost.com/entry/how-america-made-isis_b_5751876

17. http://content.time.com/time/politics/article/0,8599,1655995,00.html
18. https://www.latimes.com/nation/la-na-fbi-investigation-mateen-20160712-snap-story.html
19. https://odysee.com/@FreeKeene:2/NHexit-Historic-Hearing-CACR32:8
20. https://www.thecentersquare.com/new_hampshire/report-shows-granite-state-getting-314m-less-from-federal-government-in-spending-than-it-sends/article_dd8bc4ea-1906-11e9-936f-13aedba5897a.html
21. https://townhall.com/tipsheet/mattvespa/2015/06/06/how-many-federal-laws-are-there-again-n2009184
22. https://insidesources.com/study-finds-federal-regulations-cost-businesses-over-2-trillion/
23. https://www.worldometers.info/world-population/population-by-country
24. https://amzn.to/3we4m9W
25. https://nhipac.org/
26. https://www.shaheen.senate.gov/news/in-the-news/farmington-police-get-125000-federal-grant
27. https://libertyblock.com/portsmouth-police-given-more-drones-by-feds/
28. https://patch.com/new-hampshire/portsmouth-nh/more-police-drones-coming-portsmouth
29. https://www.concordmonitor.com/Archive/2014/07/BearCatArrives-cm-070814
30. https://www.nh.gov/safety/divisions/nhsp/newsevents/2017/20170607-new-hampton-sobriety-checkpoint.htm
31. https://listverse.com/2015/06/29/10-egregious-abuses-of-civil-asset-forfeiture/
32. https://www.law.cornell.edu/supct/cert/04-108

33. https://prisonerresource.com/federal-bureau-prisons/new-hampshire/
34. https://www.canada.ca/en/immigration-refugees-citizenship/services/new-immigrants/new-life-canada/driving.html
35. Lawrence, H. (2014). Aviation & the Role of the Government.
36. https://airandspace.si.edu/
37. Lawrence, H. (2014). Aviation & the Role of the Government.
38. U.S. Department of State. (25 July 2017). Open Skies Partnerships: Expanding the benefits of freer commercial aviation. https://www.state.gov/open-skies-partnerships-expanding-the-benefits-of-freer-commercial-aviation/
39. https://www.youtube.com/watch?v=AjTwcQYgISA
40. https://www.youtube.com/watch?v=wJVXonwWvPQ
41. https://www.youtube.com/watch?v=v0D1nVH1nX0
42. https://youtu.be/Iu_VqX6J93k?t=2574
43. https://www.history.com/this-day-in-history/fdr-takes-united-states-off-gold-standard
44. https://data.bls.gov/cgi-bin/cpicalc.pl?cost1=100&year1=191301&year2=201810
45. https://www.cnbc.com/2022/01/12/cpi-december-2021-.html
46. https://www.thestreet.com/investing/siegel-inflation-20-percent-stocks-rising
47. https://libertyblock.com/gold-backed-money-is-making-a-comeback/
48. https://smartasset.com/taxes/all-about-the-fica-tax
49. https://www.ssa.gov/pubs/EN-05-10137.pdf
50. https://givingusa.org/giving-usa-2018-americans-gave-410-02-billion-to-charity-in-2017-crossing-the-400-billion-mark-for-the-first-time/
51. https://libertyblock.com/is-taxation-outdated/
52. https://www.nhlottery.com/Where-The-Money-Goes.aspx
53. https://www.nhpr.org/nh-news/2017-09-28/n-h-liquor-commission-touts-record-698m-in-sales-over-past-fiscal-year#stream/0

54. https://www.ataoutdoormedia.com/
55. https://www.nashuanh.gov/485/Advertising
56. https://www.manchesternh.gov/Adopt-A-Site/Capital-Improvements
57. https://www.statista.com/statistics/236958/advertising-spending-in-the-us/
58. https://libertyblock.com/the-new-free-market-fund-anything-at-no-cost/
59. https://www.forbes.com/sites/jrose/2019/03/21/how-much-do-youtubers-really-make/#54b85ed67d2b
60. https://www.eia.gov/state/print.php?sid=NH
61. https://paylesspower.com/blog/electric-rates-by-state/
62. https://libertyblock.com/divorce-dc/
63. https://www.nrc.gov/
64. https://www.nrc.gov/reading-rm/doc-collections/cfr/part171/part171-0016.html
65. https://www.ecfr.gov/current/title-10/chapter-I
66. https://www.ecfr.gov/current/title-40
67. https://www.ferc.gov/industries-data/hydropower
68. https://www.ecfr.gov/current/title-18
69. https://www.nrel.gov/docs/fy16osti/66724.pdf
70. https://www.youtube.com/watch?v=WGBkV3ZLTDI
71. https://www.canadianenergycentre.ca/nearly-2-trillion-in-energy-trade-flows-between-canada-and-the-u-s-trends-from-2000-to-2019/
72. https://www.bestplaces.net/economy/state/new_hampshire
73. https://www.wmc.org/news/press-releases/federal-regs-cost-u-s-economy-more-than-2-trillion-annually-wmc-says-wisconsin-hit-harder-due-to-large-manufacturing-sector/
74. https://www.education.nh.gov/sites/g/files/ehbemt326/files/inline-documents/sonh/fall-enroll21-22.pdf
75. https://www.education.nh.gov/sites/g/files/ehbemt326/files/inline-documents/sonh/home-school21-22.pdf
76. https://www.univstats.com/states/new-hampshire/student-population

77. https://www.usgrants.org/new-hampshire/education-grants
78. https://das.nh.gov/budget/Budget2020-2021/Executive%20Summary%20Final.pdf
79. https://nhfpi.org/assets/2021/02/NHFPI-The-New-Hampshire-State-Budget-and-Education-Funding-2.11.21.pdf
80. https://das.nh.gov/budget/Budget2022-2023/Executive-Summary-FY22-23.pdf
81. https://www.govinfo.gov/app/collection/cfr/2021/title34
82. https://www.crisismagazine.com/2013/the-federal-hand-behind-common-core
83. https://www.schoolchoicenh.org/2014/12/18/why-did-nh-adopt-common-core-math-standards/
84. http://www.nysed.gov/news/2019/state-education-department-releases-spring-2019-grades-3-8-ela-math-assessment-results
85. https://www.publicschoolreview.com/blog/college-readiness-lacking-in-new-york-city-schools
86. fee.org/thinkecon/articles/the-problem-with-education-isn-t-spending
87. https://www.fs.usda.gov/whitemountain
88. https://www.fws.gov/refuge/great-bay
89. https://www.dailywire.com/news/obama-just-grabbed-millions-acres-land-utah-nevada-aaron-bandler
90. https://stacker.com/new-hampshire/see-how-much-land-new-hampshire-owned-federal-government
91. https://www.independentsentinel.com/land-grab/
92. https://www.capoliticalreview.com/capoliticalnewsandviews/obama-steals-another-1-8-million-acres-of-california-land-for-the-feds-265-million-acres-of-american-in-seven-years/
93. us-postoffice.com/nh
94. forbes.com/sites/adamandrzejewski/2021/02/20/why-the-us-post-office-is-in-trouble--678539-employees-and-a-92-billion-loss-in-2020/?sh=69cf64b2314e
95. libertyblock.com/mail-order-convenience-for-the-left

96. wikipedia.org/wiki/Congressional_Post_Office_scandal
97. peasedev.org/about
98. military.com/base-guide/browse-by-service/air-force
99. https://www.concordmonitor.com/NH-legislation-limits-federal-land-purchase-conservation-2743244
100. https://www.surveyusa.com/client/PollReport.aspx?g=f4ec3bab-2167-4e8e-ab64-671c1b4a5ddd
101. https://civiqs.com/results/track_country?uncertainty=true&annotations=true&zoomIn=true
102. https://docs.cdn.yougov.com/pst9hlpdz5/20220708_yahoo_tabs.pdf
103. https://www.fff.org/2017/09/08/sanctions-act-war/
104. bloomberg.com/news/articles/2021-05-18/best-places-to-live-moving-to-mexico-taiwan-and-costa-rica-for-quality-of-life
105. worldpopulationreview.com/country-rankings/median-income-by-country
106. libertyblock.com/newly-minted-dem-files-bill-to-kick-pro-independence-reps-from-nh-house-according-to-sources
107. https://libertyblock.com/dc-apologist-files-complaint-to-remove-pro-independence-reps-from-ballot/
108. https://libertyblock.com/breaking-nh-house-kills-legislation-to-allow-citizens-to-vote-in-independence/
109. https://amzn.to/3LqA3I8
110. gencourt.state.nh.us/RSA/html/LXII/631/631-4.htm
111. https://gencourt.state.nh.us/ethics/publications/Ethics%20Booklet%20-%20March%202020.pdf
112. https://www.youtube.com/watch?v=oBDlHiYeSec

www.ingramcontent.com/pod-product-compliance
Lightning Source LLC
Chambersburg PA
CBHW052332220526
45472CB00001B/390